THE EMPEROR'S MONK

Other books by Allen Cabaniss

Freemasonry in Mississippi (1976)
Judith Augusta: A Daughter-in-Law of Charlemagne (1974)
Charlemagne (1972)
Cabaniss Through Four Generations (1971)
Liturgy and Literature (1970)
Charlemagne's Cousins (1967)
Son of Charlemagne (1961)
Early Medieval Theology (with George E. McCracken, 1957)
Amalarius of Metz (1954)
Agobard of Lyons: Churchman and Critic (1953)
A History of the University of Mississippi (1949; 2nd ed.,
   The University of Mississippi: Its First Hundred Years, 1971)
Life and Thought of a Country Preacher (1942)

THE EMPEROR'S MONK

CONTEMPORARY LIFE OF
BENEDICT OF ANIANE
BY ARDO

Translated with an Introduction
by
Allen Cabaniss

ARTHUR H. STOCKWELL LTD.
Elms Court   Ilfracombe
Devon

ISBN 0 7223 1228-8
Printed in Great Britain by
Arthur H. Stockwell Ltd.
Elms Court   Ilfracombe
Devon

*For
Bobby, Jr.*

CONTENTS

To the Reader: An Explanation

To expedite internal reference and to avoid excessive annotation, I am resorting to the following procedure, which I hope the reader will consider before going any further in this book.

First, I have designated sections of the ensuing introduction by capital letters and each paragraph by an Arabic numeral; thus "introduction A:3" will direct one to section A and the third paragraph. In the text of the translation each paragraph of the author's preface is indicated by a lower case letter of the alphabet in parentheses, thus "(c)," meaning third paragraph of the Latin preface. I have adhered to the Latin chapter divisions but given each paragraph (which is my own decision) an Arabic numeral, if the chapter has more than one paragraph. Thus "18:2" will mean chapter 18 and the second paragraph.

Secondly, I have reserved major documentation for the introduction, some of it internal, some in separate notes. In the text, therefore, much annotation will be by reference to part of the introduction; for example, identification of persons mentioned by the Latin author.

Thirdly, the text here translated is the edition by W. Wattenbach in *Monumenta Germaniae historica*, SS

XV, Part I, pages 200-220 (introduction, 198f.), to which the reader is referred for discussion of manuscript tradition and variants.

Fourthly, in several places (by no means all) I have alluded to other saints' lives to give a few instances of the similarity that characterized most works of that genre before this life of Benedict of Aniane was written. Many of the Biblical phrases are my own discovery and are noted internally. The translation remains as faithful to the Latin as English idiom permits. I have, however, taken a liberty of supplying some proper names in place of pronouns to avoid ambiguity.

Lastly, the following recognized abbreviations of printed material are used without further mention of them:

MGH — *Monumenta Germaniae historica*
PLAC — *Poetae Latini aevi Carolini*
SS — *Scriptores*
EppKa — *Epistolae Karolini aevi*
SS. rer. Merow. — *Scriptores rerum Merowingicarum*
PL — J. P. Migne, *Patrologiae cursus completus: series Latina.*

Acknowledgements

There appears to be no previous vernacular translation of the full Ardo, *Vita Benedicti*, only of small portions; and little effort has been made to provide a narrative account of Benedict's life. There are some cursory remarks about him in Eleanor S. Duckett, *Alcuin, Friend of Charlemagne* (New York; Macmillan, 1951), and her *Carolingian Portraits* (Ann Arbor: University of Michigan Press, 1962), but nothing much beyond a summary of Ardo's *Vita*. So far as I know, there has been no successor comparable to P.J. Nicolai, *Der heilige Benedict, Gründer von Aniane und Corneli-münster, Reformator des Benedictinerordens* (Cologne, 1865), which was not available to me (the Library of Congress being authority for the assertion that it is not in the United States). Most later treatments deal with specialized aspects of Benedict's life and activities, but that is not my purpose here.

My procedure has been to make the translation and write sections A and B of the introduction before consulting any secondary material in order to arrive at a fresh, uninhibited consideration of the subject. Only then did I turn to comments by others. The notes will indicate my indebtedness, but I must single out for special mention the following:

Sigurd Abel, *Jahrbücher des fränkischen Reichs unter Karl dem Grossen*, 2 vols.: Vol. I, 2nd ed. Bernhard Simson (Leipzig: Duncker und Humblot, 1888); Vol. II, completed by Simson (1883);

Bernard S. Bachrach, "A Reassessment of Visigothic Jewish Policy, 589-711," *American Historical Review*, LXXVIII, No. 1 (Feb. 1973), 11-34; review of Zuckerman (see below), ibid., No. 5 (Dec. 1973), 1440f.;

Joseph Bédier, *Les legendes épiques: recherches sur la formation des chansons de geste*, I, *Le cycle de Guillaume d'Orange*, 3rd ed. (Paris: Édouard Champion, 1926), especially chapters 3, 4, and 5;

J.F. Böhmer, E. Mühlbacher, J. Lechner, *Die Regesten des Kaiserreichs unter den Karolingern 751-918* (Innsbruck: Verlag der Wagner'schen Universitäts-Buchhandlung, 1908);

Erich Bornmann, *Zeitrechnung und Kirchenjahr* and *Calendarium perpetuum* (Kassel: Johannes Stauda, 1964);

Wolfgang Braunfels, ed., *Karl der Grosse: Lebenswerk und Nachleben* (Düsseldorf: L. Schwann), Vols. I-III (1965), IV (1967), V (indexes, 1968), especially: Philippe Wolff, "L'Aquitaine et ses marges," I, 269-321; Wilhelm Heil, "Der Adoptianismus, Alkuin und Spanien," II, 95-155; Josef Semmler, "Karl der Grosse und das fränkische Mönchtum," II, 255-289, embodying the results of some of his earlier essays;

J. Calmette, *De Bernardo sancti Guillelmi filio (?-844)* (Toulouse: Privat, 1902);

Charles W. Jones, *Saints' Lives and Chronicles in Early England* (Ithaca, N.Y.: Cornell University Press, 1947);

Max Manitius, *Geschichte der lateinischen Literatur des Mittelalters*, I (Munich: Beck, 1911);

Wilhelm Pückert, *Aniane und Gellone* (Leipzig: Hinrichs'che Buchhandlung, 1899);

Pierre Tisset, *L'Abbaye de Gellone au diocèse de Lodève des origines au XIIIe siècle* (Paris: Recueil Sirey, 1933);

Watkin Williams, "St Benedict of Aniane," *Downside Review*, LIV (July 1936), 357-374;

J. Winandy, "L'Oeuvre monastique de saint Benoît d'Aniane," *Mélanges bénédictines* (Saint Wandrille, 1947), 235-258;

Arthur J. Zuckerman, *A Jewish Princedom in Feudal France 768-900* (New York: Columbia University Press, 1972);

Corpus consuetudinum monasticarum, I (Siegburg: F. Schmitt, 1963), 501-536, "Regula sancti Benedicti abbatis Anianensis sive Collectio capitularis," and 563-582, "Modus penitentiarum Benedicti abbatis Anianensis," both edited by J. Semmler.

My thanks go to Winston W. Way, Jr., a graduate student at Michigan State University, who drew my special attention to the subject; as always to my sister, Frances C. Stephens, who helped me with proofing, indexing, and listening to early drafts; and to my little great-nephew (to whom this book is affectionately dedicated) for frequently distracting me with his playfulness. And since this final paragraph is already sentimental, I must add still another acknowledgement: to a dear old cat that was with me for more than twenty years. Carlota (named for both Charlemagne and the ill-fated Mexican empress) often lay in my lap purring as I wrote or sprawled beside my typewriter as

I copied my work; her memory haunts me yet.

University, Miss.   A.C.
Solemnity of Our Lady
   of Guadalupe, 1978

Introduction

A. The Subject

1. From the *Vita Benedicti* by Ardo, here translated, and the letters appended to it, the following chronological data concerning its hero can be extracted. His death date is precisely given as 11 February 821, a Monday (42:5).[1] The same note states that he was in his seventies (*septuagenarius*) when he died. His birth was, therefore, about 750. A day or two before his demise he told his followers that he had been a monk for forty-eight years (42:4). Thus the year of his profession was about 773. Three years earlier than that, about 770, he was inflamed with desire to abandon secular activity and he had undertaken ascetic practices (1:2). But he delayed formal decision until "the year that Italy was made subject to the sway of glorious King Charles" (2:1). That Italian (more properly, Lombard) war was fought, as known from other sources, in 773-774.[2] Hence the previous dating is approximately accurate.

2. Before his first feeling for the religious life, Benedict was reared at the court of King Pepin (king, 751-768), Charles's father, where he ultimately became a cupbearer (*pincerna*). When he was old

enough he entered the military service of Pepin until the latter's death (768). After that and upon Charles's accession (first as joint king, then in 771 as sole king), he continued in the royal army (1:1). The age of fifteen or thereabout was a usual period at which one was girded with the sword.[3] For about five years, then, Benedict was a soldier, as his father had been before him (1:1).

3. The place of Benedict's profession as monk was the abbey of Saint Seine near Dijon (2:2). There he remained for two and a half years, according to Ardo and the letter mentioned above (2:3; 42:1). But Ardo contradicted himself, for in another passage he intimated the duration as five years and eight months (3:1). The discrepancy has been quite reasonably resolved by assuming the two and a half years to refer to Benedict's monastic experience before he was appointed cellarer and the five and two thirds years to the whole time elapsed since his profession.[4] Benedict therefore left Saint Seine about 779.

4. Another fairly definite date in the *Vita* emerges by allusion to a "very severe" (*gravissima*) famine (7:1). That could be the one (*vero magna*) mentioned in the annals of Lorsch for 779.[5] But it was more likely the one of 793 (*validissima*) recorded in the chronicle of Moissac,[6] because of the statement, "at the same time the baneful doctrine of Felicianism" invaded the Midi (8:1). That is known to have occurred during the interval 789-792.[7] Felix abjured his erroneous teaching in 792, but in 793 relapsed into it, eluded his jailers, and fled to Muslim Spain.[8] The *Vita* is in consequence probably correct in stating that the famine and the heresy occurred "at the same time" (7:1; 8:1).

5. Three other dates are given: one, explicitly; the others, by inference. The first was 782, the year in which Benedict undertook an expansive building program for Aniane (17:2). It was particularly important because he changed his style completely: whereas he had in the past allowed only the crudest structures (5:2), he now unaccountably permitted elaborate and rich ornamentation (17:2). The second date, ten years later, is implied. Embedded in the *Vita* (18:3-6) is a text of "immunity" granted by Charles to Benedict and Aniane.[9] Another royal charter, confirming to Benedict the estate of Celleneuve, dated June 799,[10] is also suggested, but there is no certainty about it (19:1). The third date, 816-818, is indicated by reference to a great assembly at Aix,[11] an effort to bring some degree of uniformity to monastic practice in the Carolingian domain, an action that seemed to be an imperial attempt to set Benedict "over all the monasteries" in the realm (36:1).

6. In addition to chronological data, the *Vita* offers the following about its protagonist. He was born in Gothia "of the nation of the Getae" and "of noble origin." His father (unnamed) was a count of Maguelonne,[12] a loyal adherent of the Frankish government and an effective military chieftain, noted especially for his crushing defeat of marauding Basques. He entrusted his young son to King Pepin's court. There Benedict was one of "the queen's [Bertrada's] scholars," beloved by his peers in age, nimble-witted, and adaptable. Rising to prominence in such surroundings, he entered those military duties expected of a youth of his status (1:1).

7. About the age of twenty Benedict was for some reason attracted to religious life. Although he

B

continued to perform his secular obligations, he brooded over the strong appeal of religion and began to practice austerities (1:2). Uncertain of the effect of an open decision on his father, he hesitated about the particular future expression of his desire. Among the possibilities were to become a lifelong pilgrim, to become a shepherd or herdsman in the countryside without pay, or to become a shoemaker[13] in some city, sustaining his work among the poor by the labor of his hands (1:3).

8. The event that forced him to a decision was an encounter with death. He witnessed his brother trying recklessly to ford a raging river, presumably in northern Italy. Riding into the flood in an attempt (whether successful, we are not informed) to rescue his brother, Benedict himself was almost drowned. In the narrow escape Benedict, like Martin Luther over seven centuries later, vowed to abandon the world. At once he returned to his home land (2:1). Still hesitant to discuss his problem with his father, he confided in a blind solitary named Widmar, who was able to advise him, yet maintain the secret. In an act of deception comparable to Bodo-Eleazar's more than fifty years later,[14] Benedict made ostensible plans to go to Aix-la-Chapelle and appear before King Charles. But when he and his companions reached the community of Saint Seine, he suddenly threw off the cloak of secrecy, dismissed his escort, and in due course made profession as monk (2:2).

9. During the time at Saint Seine, perhaps five and two thirds years (3:1), less likely two and a half (2:3), Benedict practiced excessive fasting, weeping, sleeplessness, and prayer (2:3-5). He performed menial tasks for his brothers, wore the meanest garments,

avoided bathing, and allowed his body to be covered by lice which gnawed at his poor flesh (2:4). The abbot tried to persuade, even compel, him to moderate his rigor. But Benedict churlishly declared that the famous *Rule* of the man whose name he bore was fit for novices and weaklings who were capable merely of doing things within the realm of possibility (2:5). He himself preferred, so he said, the harsher precepts of Basil (ca. 329-379, metropolitan of Cappadocian Caesarea) and Pachomius (292-346, of Egypt, author of the first known cenobitical rule), who advocated striving to achieve impossible things. Not content to practice austerities in private, he took it upon himself publicly to challenge the manners of his fellows, to scold, exhort, admonish, and upbraid (2:3-5).

10. For a while he served the community as cellarer. That office afforded him opportunity to commit the Benedictine *Rule* to memory, a feat which probably led him to relax attachment to the life prescribed by his Eastern mentors. All the while he took his duty seriously. In distribution he was generous to those who sought in what he deemed a lawful manner, but refused those who sought "unlawfully." For that reason he fell into disfavor with many of the brothers. Yet in providing for guests, children, and poor folk, he exercised gentle care and the abbot was quite fond of him (2:6).

11. It was apparently during Benedict's "tour" as cellarer that the abbot died. Despite his style of life, there was a perverse demand by the brothers for him to become abbot. But when he assessed the situation, he decided wisely that there would be sharp internal strife. In his awareness Benedict was more discreet than Peter Abelard as abbot of Saint Gildas was at a

20

later time. As hurriedly as he had gone to and entered Saint Seine, he now deserted it and returned to his father's estates. There, on the banks of a stream called Aniane, near the Saône river, he, about thirty years of age, and a few like-minded companions (including Widmar, the blind solitary) erected a hut so they could dwell near a small church of Saint Saturninus (3:1). He and his community lived, worked, and prayed there in deepest poverty. Kindly women of the neighbourhood occasionally brought them milk and nearby clergy gave them encouragement (3:1-3; 4:2). Benedict is said to have baked bread for his followers and to have hauled wood on his own shoulders to construction sites, but also to have found opportunity to write a book (5:1), to preach to and instruct the brothers (4:1), and to say Mass (5:1, 3; 21:1). When and where he received Holy Orders is not indicated in the *Vita*, but in the mid-820s Ermoldus Nigellus referred to the late Benedict as *sacerdos* (priest).[15]

12. With passage of time the community grew so that more and more buildings were required. Benedict insisted on the cheapest timber, thatched roofs, and no ornamentation (5:2). But as Aniane's reputation for holiness and good works spread (5:1), with fame came also fortune. People began to bestow land and wealth upon the foundation (5:3; 6; 17:2), and, as noted earlier, a subtle change took place in Benedict. About his thirty-second or thirty-third year he began to sponsor sumptuous buildings (17:2). One monastic church is described glowingly by Ardo (17:3) in terms that anticipate Abbot Suger's boasts about the treasures of Saint Denis.[16] It was covered with red tiles, not thatch; it had painted panelings; and marble columns to sustain the cloister porches (5:2; 17:2).

Multiple altars, lamps, and candelabra, intricately contrived, are mentioned (17:3-6). An important library was assembled as well as costly vestments and silver vessels. It was a school for cantors and lectors, for grammarians and Scripture scholars.[17] Indeed several of Benedict's students were elevated to the episcopate (18:1).

13. Looking back over his life thus far we may logically discern three "conversions" that Benedict underwent. The first, his "evangelical" experience, was an emotional shift from secular to religious interests about 770 (1:2); the second, his monastic profession about 774 (2:2); and the third, his relaxation of rigorism about 782 (17:2; 21:1). His biographer considered the last a decline (*declinarat*, 21:1), but we may perhaps deem it an intellectual change.

14. Benedict's several "conversions" were reflected in his attitude toward the famous *Rule*. At his first conversion, while still wondering what to do with his life, he fell in love with it, but at Saint Seine he tended to denigrate it in comparison with the more severe Eastern rules. Yet he was unable to abandon his attachment to it and during his time as cellarer memorized it (2:6). When he became the superior of an ever increasing number of monasteries, he devoted himself to intensive study and mastery of the *Rule*, visiting various communities to inquire of experts what he did not know or understand. For the sake of comparison, he assembled a library of as many different rules as he could discover (18:1). In his visits Benedict made a practice of explaining obscurities in it (20). As a result his followers were steeped in its teaching and discipline.

15. At King Louis's insistence, Benedict traveled throughout Aquitaine reviving the *Rule* where it had fallen into desuetude (18:1; 29:1). So often did he visit many monasteries to discuss it chapter by chapter, that it is no wonder numerous counts accused him of being "a wandering monk" (29:3). After Louis's accession to the empire, Benedict was responsible for revival of the *Rule* in Frankland (35; 36:1). He played a leading role at the council of Aix (816-818) by his expositions (36:1). The *Rule*, it was said, was his greatest study. He made a practice of interrogating scholars both near at hand and at a distance (18:1; 38:6). Visitors on their way to Monte Cassino were asked to note both what they heard and what they saw, then report to him (38:6). Finally he compiled a book, *Concordia regularum* (A Harmony of the Rules), quoting passages from other rules to show the superiority of Saint Benedict's (38:7).

16. By 792 Aniane was head of a family of monastic communities, not only in Gothia, but also in other parts of the Carolingian world (18:1). Ten years earlier King Charles had already granted significant "immunity" to Aniane and its complex (18:3-6); he continued to do so as late as 799 (19:1), by which time he may have been involved in his imperial adventure. As early as 792 or thereabout Benedict, too, was deeply embroiled in extra-monastic activity. He and others were, for instance, busily engaged in campaigning in southern Gaul and perhaps Spain against Felix of Urgel and his teaching (8:1). Because of his varied labors and the reputation of his monks for sanctity, Benedict was well known among all classes. The turn from the rigor of his first way of life, while perhaps disappointing to his biographer, was nonetheless

recognized by Ardo as necessary because "he had undertaken an impossible task." But Benedict's purpose remained, so he plowed, dug, and reaped along with others (21:1). He maintained his abstinence from meat and wine, except when he was ill; he then took some chicken broth (21:2). He also pursued in an unusual manner his pastoral care, being able to cure others of the typical monastic malaise of *acedia* or melancholy (21:4).

17. The fame of his monks had become so widespread that eminent prelates asked for some of them to inaugurate, to strengthen, or to reform their own communities. Among them, Bishop Leidrad of Lyons, Bishop Theodulf of Orléans, and Abbot Alcuin of Saint Martin at Tours sought his students (24:1, 2, 5). In 814 and afterwards Louis, originally king of Aquitaine, but then successor of his father as "emperor of the whole church in Europe" (29:1), having already discovered Benedict's way of holiness (19:2; 31:1; 33; 34), "set him over all the monasteries in the realm" (29:1). Good Queen Irmingard, too, admired him (31:1). As a result Benedict was summoned to Marmoutier in Alsace. Even that place was not close enough to Louis, so the emperor removed him to a small new monastic settlement on the river Inde very near Aix-la-Chapelle. Thus Benedict could always be available for consultation at the palace (35:1, 2).

18. Despite Benedict's powerful friends, the *Vita* did not neglect his enemies. The earliest were his fellows at Saint Seine, whom he irritated with his exceptional austerities (2:4). Others were some of his own students at Aniane (3:2; 10; 16).[18] Still others were sneering layfolk who despised his movement (26; 29:3). As Benedict advanced in public esteem, some of

24

the secular clergy tried to minimize his activities. Some of the nobility, envious of his position, condemned him as a vagabond, greedy for property (29:3). But before his death his friends outnumbered his enemies in influence and importance.

19. It is worthy of note that the *Vita* does not gloss over certain aspects of its hero's life that were not admirable. To us perhaps the most unfavorable feature was Benedict's physical filthiness: the few baths during his lifetime, his body crawling with lice, and his refusal to change clothes more often than at forty-day intervals (2:4; 43:2). Even Ardo remarked that his theadbare, patched cowls "rendered him somewhat unsightly" (2:4). His extreme "finickiness" in eating must have been a trial to those in the kitchen of his monastery (21:2, 3) and his habit of scolding did not help (2:5). His sharp disagreement with his abbot at Saint Seine did not set a good example (2:5); in fact the word to describe it is *churlish*. Ecstatics he looked upon as rude (9), a strange description coming from Benedict. Even in his own day his manner of life was deemed new and strange (3:2), and Benedict's disgust with those who did not persevere in it was not encouraging.

20. When time came for a change, it was left unexplained in the *Vita*. Some of it was attributed to his realization of impossibilities involved in his earlier way (17:2; 21:1). Some of it was indeed compromise for the sake not only of human frailty, but also for the sake of appearance (37:2) — a curious characterization of the austere Benedict, but perhaps experience was having a didactic effect. It is significant that his religious life had begun in deception (2:1, 2). Apparently he misled his father and many of his

companions when he undertook monastic conversion.

21. From the first years of Louis's reign as emperor Benedict's constant attendance on him caused his biographer to state that he wore "away the palace floors." All who suffered injuries from others or who sought imperial opinions used him as intermediary (35:3). Many laymen besieged him with questions "about direction of the realm, about disposition of provinces, and about their own advantage." But Benedict, although desirous of assisting everyone, gave his primary attention to the needs of monks (35:4). By that time he had become a devoted advocate of the moderate *Rule* of Saint Benedict (37:2). Even as he interpreted it, however, he showed willingness to make concessions and compromises (36:1; 37; 38), and indeed to contrive devotional practices not mentioned in the *Rule* (38).[19] He made special effort, at least partially successful, to free monasteries and their communities from lay usurpation and sequestration (39).

22. During his last five years (42:5) Benedict's vigils, tears, fasting, reading, and meditation (41:1), as surely the physical exertion noted above, and the oversight of twelve communities (42:2),[20] together with lack of cleanliness (41:2), took their toll on his life and he began to waste away. His final illness started on 7 and 8 February 821 (42:3; 43:4). On 9 February he was removed from his room at Aix to his monastery of Inde (42:4), where on 11 February, first Monday of Lent, he died surrounded by his followers. Two days later (that is, "on the third day") he was buried there in a stone sepulcher ordered by Emperor Louis (42:5).

23. In the *Vita* there are numerous references to writings by Benedict, few of which have survived. The

first was an unidentified work done early in his career while cooking in the kitchen (5:1). The second was a collection of all the rules he could discover (this may allude to the gathering of a library, 18:1). The third was Benedict's compilation of a decree for the emperor's seal, summarizing action of the council of Aix that strove to bring monastic uniformity in Frankland (38:6). The fourth was a letter to Louis concerning the *Rule* (ibid.). The fifth was a compilation (under Benedict's direction) from the rules of various Fathers to be read at the morning assembly (38:7). The sixth was another book called *Concordia regularum* (ibid.). The seventh was still another compiled from the "sermons of holy teachers" to be read at the evening assemblies (ibid.). Finally there was a record, found after his death, of "every office he had performed during the five years and two months" preceding his decease (42:5). It is an amazing list, suggesting the important intellectual interest and equipment of the man.

24. The foregoing paragraphs constitute the life of Benedict as derived from Ardo's account. For further data one must have recourse to sources apart from the *Vita*, but they are sparse, only "some small islands . . . that emerge here and there in an ocean of forgetfulness and silence."[21] Of interest, however, we find that his name before profession was Vitiza (or Witiza). It must have been employed occasionally after profession, for it was given in the chronicle of Moissac at the year 794, recording his presence in Frankfurt at the council which debated the issues of Felicianism and images. The statement is *Benedictus qui vocatur Vitiza* (Benedict who is called Vitiza — note the present tense of the verb).[22] Vitiza may be the name Latinized to

Euticius in the *Vita*, I, 23, of Saint Odo (ca. 879-942), second abbot of Cluny, as the one for whom Emperor Louis erected a monastery near the palace,[23] unless indeed *Euticius* (*Eutychius*) is a Hellenized version of *Benedictus* (both words mean *fortunate*). He may, of course, have been named for one of the last Visigothic kings of Spain (Witiza, 700-710).[24]

25. Additional facts are derived from the correspondence of Alcuin (ca. 735-804), abbot of Saint Martin.[25] He and Benedict were friends before the former went to Tours (796). Not only did Benedict offer prayers for Alcuin, but also sent him some medicinal herbs for which the latter dispatched a note of thanks.[26] Alcuin also submitted some of his letters for Benedict's comments and for delivery to the appropriate persons, one indeed to King Charles.[27] After Alcuin became abbot of Saint Martin, he founded a new congregation about eight miles away (at Cormery, so we learn from Ardo's *Vita*, 24:5), the first contingent of monks being some he had requested from Benedict's care — this in a letter to his friend, Bishop Arno of Salzburg.[28] In 800 he wrote to Leidrad, bishop of Lyons (799-815), Nibridius, abbot of La Grasse, then bishop of Narbonne (ca. 799-ca. 822), and Benedict concerning a new journey they were undertaking, on Charles's order, to preach against the Felician heresy in the area between the Loire and Ebro rivers.[29] From it we learn that it was the second such trip the three had made. Shortly thereafter Alcuin wrote another letter to the same three on the same subject.[30] After that came a letter to all the monastic establishments of Gothia. In it he discussed a book he had written against the heresy and which he had transmitted to them by Abbot Benedict.[31] Then

28

he sent a letter to Nibridius commending Benedict
with whom he had just talked and who was then on his
way to Nibridius.[32] Almost immediately a letter went
to his friend Arno. It told of Felix's imprisonment at
Lyons and of the three clerics' visit *in illas partes
occidentales* (into those western regions) to extinguish
the faithless doctrine.[33]

26. The author of Alcuin's life related that Benedict
visited Alcuin for counsel concerning his own salvation
and that of his students in Gothia. Alcuin is supposed
to have been able clairvoyantly to anticipate Benedict's
approach and to have sent forward an escort to
accompany him, but he declined to satisfy Benedict's
curiosity about the occurrence. The two men were so
intimate that Alcuin revealed to Benedict his own
special private prayer and Benedict presumed to
suggest an additional petition, to which the former
happily replied, "So be it, most revered son, so be
it."[34] The author advised those who could not follow
in the steps of the ancient churchmen to follow those
who lived more recently, who were approved by Christ,
and who were worthy of imitation, namely, "for monks
Benedict [of Aniane] and for canons Alcuin."[35]

27. Theodulf (ca. 750-821), bishop of Orléans,
wrote a poem for Aniane's monks and Benedict.[36] To
the latter he declared, "What Benedict [of Nursia] was
as director in Italian lands, so you, Benedict [of
Aniane], are in our lands."[37] He asked for assistance
and Benedict dispatched two monks (line 11). So
successful were they that Benedict later sent him "twice
ten" 24:2. Theodulf added some other names of
Benedict's friends (that is, other than himself,
Nibridius, Atilio, abbot of Saint Thibéry, and
Anianus, abbot of Saints John and Lawrence, 3:1):

Donatus (line 68); Nampius or Nampio (line 71), abbot of Saint Hilary near Carcassonne; Orlemundus (line 72), abbot of Montolieu; Clarinus, Teutfredus, and Leubila (line 77). He mentioned Atilius (line 77; presumably the same as Atilio, 3:1, 3), Atala (line 72), and Attila (line 77; the latter two also perhaps the same as Atilio, or was Atala the abbot from Spain in whose company Agobard came to Septimania?)[38]

28. To complete the list it may be fitting to note the persons mentioned in Ardo's *Vita* as Benedict's acquaintances in one way or another. By name we have Ardo (d. 843; see 16; 21:2; introduction B), Helisachar, abbot of Saint Riquier and imperial chancellor (i; 42:3; 43:4),[39] King Pepin (1:1), King (Emperor) Charles (1:1; 18:1),[40] blind Widmar (2:2; 3:1), Atilio (3:1, 3), Nibridius (3:1; 44:1), Anianus (3:1), Leidrad (24:1), Theodulf (24:2), Alcuin (24:5), Louis the Pious (29:1; 42:2),[41] Andoar (31:1), Wulfar (a relative of William of Gellone; 34; cf. 30 and introduction C), Stabilis, bishop of Maguelonne (41:4), Tanculf, chief of the royal fisc (42:4),[42] Deidonus, Leovigild, Bertrad, Desiderius (42:6), George, third abbot of Aniane, 819-822 (43:1), and Modan (43:3). Six persons are mentioned but not by name: Benedict's father (1:1), Queen Bertrada, mother of Charlemagne (d. 783; 1:1), Benedict's brother (2:1), the abbot of Saint Seine (2:6), Felix, heretic bishop of Urgel (8:1),[43] and Empress Irmingard (d. 818), first wife of Louis the Pious, or possibly Empress Judith (ca. 805-844),[44] Louis's second wife (31:4; 42:3).

29. Benedict's compilations that have survived are a collection of rules (part I, of Eastern Fathers; part II, of Western Fathers; and part III, for nuns)[45] and the

30

Concordia regularum.[46] Imperial charters issued in favor of Aniane during Benedict's lifetime were one by Charles and nine by Louis.[47]

30. Only three letters by Benedict are extant. One, to his student Guarnarius, was written about the time of Felician activity.[48] The student, otherwise unknown, seems to have fallen into that heresy, but the evidence is not conclusive. The note is a miscellany of passages from Scripture along with one from Isidore (ca. 560-636), bishop of Seville, one from Augustine (354-430), bishop of Hippo, and one from Leo I (pope, 440-461), together with allusion to a formula of faith that Benedict had written. The other two, appended to the *Vita,* were written (dictated) on the eve of his death: one, to Abbot George of Aniane, encouraging him to keep up his good work and to consider Abbot Helisachar a trustworthy friend (43); the other, to Bishop Nibridius, asking him to continue his kindly interest in Aniane (44).

31. Reactions to the life and work of Benedict of Aniane varied, as we have seen, in his lifetime. Within the last century they are expressed, on one hand, by Edmund Bishop, "After the great founder himself, Benedict of Nursia, no man has more widely affected Western monachism than did the second Benedict, he of Aniane"[49]; on the other, by David Knowles's comment on that judgment, "This is put strongly, perhaps too strongly, for the two differed in kind as well as in degree; Benedict of Aniane has never been a spiritual guide for monks."[50]

B. The Author and Text

1. After Benedict's death some of his associates at

Inde, namely, Deidonus, Leovigild, Bertrad, and Desiderius, addressed a letter to Ardo, teacher and monk of Aniane, requesting him to compose Benedict's *Vita* (42). With the letter they sent along some notes they had assembled about their late abbot (f; 42:6). Exact date of that communication is not known. Calling himself "a slave of Messiah's servants" (a), almost the title employed by Pope Gregory the Great, Ardo stated that, by the time he began to prepare the *Vita*, it was "a long time ago" (*iam pridem*) that the letter was delivered to him (b). At first Ardo demurred, feeling humility as well as his lack of urbanity, ability, and training (a, b, e). He hoped that someone better qualified would undertake the task (d). The brothers, however, importuned him (f). In addition there was a certain sentimental aura at Aniane, Benedict's original foundation, that affected Ardo (or so he intimated) and impelled him to acquiesce in the request (f). Still further, Abbot Helisachar was apparently urging him (i). And there was, despite some timidity, a genuine scholarly impulse to write. Ardo was aware that in the lay world matters and events were recorded for future generations. So in the religious world there was need for the same thing lest "obliging forgetfulness and scurrying time" obliterate important occurrences from memory (j). So he finally assumed the task.

2. In the work Ardo gave only a glimpse of his own life. He was correct when he alluded to his crudity of language (e, g, k): among other matters, employment of accusatives absolute or mixed with ablatives absolute, prepositions with the wrong case, corrupt forms (*equites* for *equos*, for example). The solecisms, apparent in his Latin text, are certainly not unusual

for his time and place. He was quite capable of conveying his thoughts adequately. There is no parade of literary virtuosity. A few references to Virgil appear in his *praefatio* (d) and perhaps at 5:1. Throughout the book occur constant citations of Scripture. Ardo was familiar with the interior life of monastic communities and also with the usual content of saints' lives. But of the latter it is difficult to ascertain with precision any particular ones that he had read.

3. Ardo claimed personal knowledge of his hero and of a number of incidents that he had witnessed (e.g., 16; 17; 21:2; 25:3; 28:2; 31:3, etc.) Nor did he hesitate to report occasional unfavorable reactions to Benedict. But he had only fleeting glimpses of the abbot in the great secular world and of his powerful impact upon it. A single note seems quite revealing: it is a vivid picture which Ardo secured from some source and which has two items of interest. First is Benedict's procedure when agreeing to intercede with the emperor for various persons. We observe how modern it was when he caused complaints to be reduced to writing (35:3). Second is the vignette of Louis receiving them. He sat or stood, nervously plucking at his sleeves or a napkin, reading them in order of receipt. When familiarized with the problems presented, Louis made judgment as usefully as he could. But sometimes he wearily shoved them aside and forgot them until prodded by Benedict (35:3).

4. Externally the text of Ardo's *Vita* contains a *praefatio* and forty-one chapters, as well as a collection of three letters and a few notes at the end. Chapter 30, however, is an interpolation not earlier than the eleventh century. It purports to be a brief life of William of Gellone. Skillfully constructed to appear an

original part of the *Vita Benedicti*, its first sentence ties well to the end of chapter 29:4; the last sentence of 30:5 tries to make transition to chapter 31 easy not by repeating the exact words of 28:2, "Let us return to the sequence we began," but by adding the word *rursus*, "Let us *again* return . . ." (30:5). Whoever composed the chapter attempted to convey verisimilitude by one first-personal remark, "I think it worthwhile to relate . . ." (30:3). The rest of the text bears little relation to the story of Benedict; and moreover, except for one slight allusion (34), Benedict's *Vita* makes no reference to William either before or after the insertion. If chapter 30 is ignored, the flow from the last sentence of chapter 29 to the first of chapter 31 is unbroken.

5. Apart from that there are inserted thirteen accounts of miracles (12:2; 13; 14; 15; 23; 24:3, 4; 25:3; 26; 27:1; 27:2; 28:1; 31:3; 32). The first four are contiguous and introduced as miracles, "Since almighty God . . . performs on suitable occasions miracles through His servants, I will compress into a brief narrative some that He did through Benedict" (12:1). They are concluded with a humorous incident known personally to Ardo (16). The fifth and sixth are fairly contiguous, but not introduced as miracles, only as incidents derived from Ardo's investigations (24:4), the fifth being semi-humorous. The seventh through the eleventh are contiguous and are properly introduced, "I do not think it amiss if miracles . . . are inserted in this treatment" (25:1); and also concluded, "Let it suffice to have said these few things about miracles done in our time" (28:2). The twelfth and thirteenth are contiguous, but not introduced or concluded as miracles. It seems therefore apparent

C

34

that the brothers at Inde sent along with their letter some appropriate miracle stories involving Benedict which Ardo felt obliged to use.

6. Only seven of them (12:2; 13; 14; 15; 24:3, 4; 31:3; 32) are credited to Benedict himself; the remainder, to prayers by all the brothers (23; 26; 27:1; 27:2), to a relic of the cross (25:3), and to presence in a particular oratory (28:1). The last may indeed not be deemed a miracle. Only one of the thirteen (31:3) has the earmarks of a genuine violation of natural law and Ardo told none of the stories with zest. Some he attributed to his own knowledge or investigation (24:3, 4; 25:3; 31:3), not to information provided by another source. He certainly did not rely on them as of importance to the *Vita*.

7. For date of the *Vita* the *terminus a quo* is 821, Benedict's death, and the *terminus ad quem* is 840, death of Louis the Pious who is always referred to as living.[51] It must have been no later than 822 when the brothers of Inde collected their notes for Ardo. The latter waited a year, thus 823, before accepting the commission. Thereupon ensued a period of composition which required time. Hence the earliest date for the *Vita* could be 824. In the book there are no allusions to the troubled years of 830-833 when the Carolingian court was wracked with intrigue and rebellion[52] (not that the writer had any reason to make such allusions!) The biography was, moreover, written while persons who had known Abbot Benedict and his activities were still alive (31:3). And the pressure on Ardo to write was heavy. It would seem, therefore, appropriate to assign the *Vita* to an interval not earlier than 824 and not later than 830.

8. But it is possible to narrow the period to 824-826.

Ermoldus Nigellus's poem in honor of Emperor Louis may be dated about 827[53] and it seems entirely possible, even likely, that Ermoldus alluded to Ardo's *Vita*. The poem's description of Benedict has been denominated "stereotyped," conveying "to the mind little that can be called characteristic."[54] It does indeed make numerous literary allusions, duly indicated by Ernst Dümmler in his edition.[55] Yet no one can question aptness of the language despite its borrowings: it is as though Ermoldus had read Ardo's *Vita* and tried to improve its terminology. For example, line 533, *Vir Benedictus erat cognomine dignus eodem* (Benedict was a man worthy of his name), has in it two scarcely significant words, *cognomine dignus*, annotated as from Ovid, *Ex Ponto*, II, 5, 49. In spirit, however, as well as in words, it is similar to Ardo, *Vir venerabilis nomine et merito Benedictus* (The venerable man by name and merit Benedict — that is, "blessed one," 1:1).

9. Ermoldus's line 535, *Hic erat in Geticis regi prius agnitus*[56] *arvis* (He was known[57] in 'Getic' fields before the king), annotated by citation of Vergil, *Aeneid*, III, 35, *Geticus qui praesidet arvis* (He who presides over 'Getic' fields), and Ovid, *Ex Ponto*, I, 9, 45, *Geticis . . . ab arvis* (from 'Getic' fields), is simply a "glamorised" version of Ardo, *Benedictus abbas ex Getarum genere partibus Gotiae oriundus* (Abbot Benedict was sprung from the nation of 'Getae' in the areas of Gothia, 1:1). Line 536, *De cuius vita pauca referre libet* (It is appropriate to relate a few things about his life) is glossed with two words from Vergil, *Aeneid*, IV, 333, *pauca refert* (he relates a few things), hardly a significant allusion, being so commonplace (this verse will, however, be adverted to again below). Line 546,

36

regula cuius erat pectore fixa sacro (whose *Rule* was fixed in his holy breast), perhaps related verbally to Ovid, *Metamorphoses*, VI, 227, *medioque in pectore fixa* (and fixed in the midst of his breast), is another "improvement" of Ardo, *quo memoriae regulam praefati patris commendavit* (where he committed to memory the *Rule* of the aforesaid Father, 2:6).

10. Other important lines from Ermoldus's poem have no classical overtones, but seem to be directly from Ardo. In line 538 the word *abba* (instead of *abbas*) is used; so also at three points in the *Vita*: 32, 35:2, and 37:2, each time with the adjective *venerabilis*. In my translation, to differentiate it from *abbas* (which I render *abbot*), I have retained the Aramaic *abba* to call attention to it. In line 541 Ermoldus used three nouns to describe Benedict, *fuit . . . norma exemplumque magister* (he was . . . a standard, an example, a teacher). Precisely those three words were also employed by Ardo: *norma* (18:1; 33; 36:2); *exemplum* (36:1); and *magister* (20; 24:3).

11. Ermoldus's line 588 spoke of the abbey of Inde as *nomen aquae retinens* (keeping the name of the stream); Ardo phrased it thus, *mutuato de rivulo eiusdem vallis nomen* (the name of the valley itself . . . derived from the little river, 35:2). According to line 589 of Ermoldus, who knew the locale, *Milibus hic ternis regali distat ab aula* (It was three miles from the royal palace); Ardo, who did not know the locale, observed, *Vallis autem erat vicina, quae a palatio (ut reor) sex non amplius milibus distat* (There was a neighboring valley which is, *I think*, not more than six miles from the palace, 35:2; emphasis added).[58] Ermoldus's line 598 is interesting, *Hludowicus adest Caesar et abba* (Louis is present as both emperor and

abba — or 'abbot'). The brothers recorded that after Benedict's death and even as they were writing, Louis *abbatem se monasterii illius palam esse profitetur* (openly declared himself *abba* — or 'abbot' — of that monastery, that is, Inde, 42:2. The words *abba* and *abbas* can have the same accusative, *abbatem*.) Ermoldus stated in line 580, *Hoc mandarentur menbra sepulta loco* (that his body would be ordered buried in this place); Ardo included a note from the brothers of Inde that Benedict was interred in a stone coffin *quod imperator paraverat* (that the emperor had had prepared, 42:5).

12. Let us now return to Ermoldus's line 536, cited above. There it was deliberately given a neutral translation so as not to prejudge the case before evidence was presented. But in view of the relation between Ermoldus's lines and Ardo's treatment, in view of the strong possibility that Ermoldus knew Ardo's work, I suggest that a more accurate version would be, "It is appropriate to mention a few things from his [Benedict's] *Vita*."

C. William of Gellone

1. For the purpose of this treatment of Benedict of Aniane, it is not necessary to add to the extensive literature on William of Gellone. For our purpose indeed it would be better to ignore the interpolated chapter 30. But some comments are perhaps in order simply to acknowledge a problem. The latest study in English is A.J. Zuckerman, *A Jewish Princedom*, already mentioned in the notes. It relies heavily on Pückert, *Aniane und Gellone*,[59] and Tisset, *L'Abbaye de Gellone*.[60] There are also some sections of Bedier,

38

Les legendes épiques, I,[61] that contribute to the subject. But I restrict my remarks to the presentation by Zuckerman as embodying the others. His book is, by the way, quite impressive, but it has not yet received the close consideration that is due to it.[62] Perhaps that will come in time.

2. Some elements of the description of William of Gellone in the interpolated chapter, although late, are based on authentic material. He was described by the writer as an eminent and favorite court official of Charles (30:1). About 846, twenty-five years after William's death, Paschasius Radbertus characterized him as "a most noble and high-minded man" and mentioned that Abbot Wala (ca. 773-834) was at one time his son-in-law.[63] At some point also William became a profound admirer of Benedict (30:1). He was indeed of noble origin (30:2), related to Charles and Louis, but the precise kinship is disputed.[64] The traditional date of his conversion is given as 29 June [806], feast of Saints Peter and Paul (30:1).[65]

3. Some problems suggested by Zuckerman[66] can be disposed of quickly. (a) There is no inner contradiction in the assertion, "with the aid of his sons whom he had set over (*praefecerat*) his counties" (30:3).[67] Note the pluperfect tense: obviously William "had set" his sons before he himself made any renunciations. (b) Zuckerman's similarities between the monastic lives of Benedict and William are commonplaces in biographies of saints and require no extended demonstration.[68] (c) Benedict's observance of both Sabbath (Saturday) and Lord's Day (Sunday) (21:2) simply reflect his documented attachment to Eastern practices where both days were (are) liturgically commemorated.[69] In fact the Western

church also observed (observes) both days, formerly Saturday in honor of the Blessed Virgin Mary, today as the Saturday vigil, the late Mass of which has the status of Sunday Mass. Moreover most Romance languages adopted the medieval and liturgical Latin term for Saturday, namely, *sabbatum*; for example, Spanish *sábado* and French *samedi*.

4. (d) Benedict maintained his abstinence from quadruped meat even in illness: it was a chicken broth (*ius e pullo compositum*, 21:2), not a *beef* broth, that he allowed himself.[70] (e) It was Louis the Pious, not William, who endowed Gellone with "silver and gold chalices and vessels for the offertory" (30:4).[71] (f) Benedict was hardly "in flight" from Saint Seine to another monastery:[72] "he hurriedly set out toward his paternal soil" (3:1) to avoid election as abbot of Saint Seine, a not infrequent occurrence during the Middle Ages. (g) It is not so obvious that he was "without possessions comparable to" those of William,[73] for Ardo remarked that he built Aniane on "property belonging to his father *and himself*" (3:1; emphasis added).

5. (h) Hebraisms in any context are the stock in trade of a hagiologist and need not detain us.[74] (i) The "archaic" word *consul* for a Frankish official was employed about 846 by Paschasius Radbertus long before any "revival [of the term] in the eleventh century."[75] Paschasius also used a more "archaic" word, *senator*, a number of times.[76] (j) The story about a fasting girl in 823-825 made no allusion to "her confirmation Mass."[77]

6. But important questions raised by Zuckerman remain. Six statements in the interpolated chapter are, at least, strange. (a) It remarks that "Permission to be

converted was finally received" (*acceptamque tandem convertendi licentia*, 30:1). Consent by the ruler for a great noble to become a monk was not unusual at that time, but the statement is followed by (b) William's gift of extensive treasure to Benedict, (c) his hasty tonsure (*nec mora*), (d) his putting off cloth-of-gold vesture, (e) then his acceptance of "the habit of Christians" (*christicolarum*), and lastly (f) his expression of gratitude that he was now numbered with the company of "heaven-dwellers" (*caelicolarum*) (30:1). When Benedict, who was also of noble origin, became a monk, there was no mention of any "permission to be converted," only to "permission to enter," granted by the community of Saint Seine (2:2). Then followed his tonsure, not hastily, as in the case of William, but in due course (*mox*). And it was said that he assumed "the vesture of a true monk" (*veri monachi abitum*, 2:2).

7. Despite similarities, the two accounts are notably different. (a) Permission was for two different aspects of a new life. (b) The source of consent for William is not indicated, as it is for Benedict. (c) In one case the tonsure was hurried; in the other, apparently after a suitable interval. (d) The "habit" of each is differently described, the more ordinary expression being for that of Benedict.

8. The Latin word for "Christians" in the William chapter is *christicolae*, not *Christiani*. Both Latin words were occasionally employed to signify *monks*, as also was the term "heaven-dwellers" (*caelicolarum*), although the latter could quite naturally mean "angels." Those words appear nowhere else in Ardo's *Vita*, but both occurred in the famed Saint Gall *Quem-quaeritis* trope near the end of the ninth

century.[79] There the former meant "Christian"; the latter, "angels." In connection with William it is entirely possible that the two words were introduced for the sake of an internal prose rhyme:

> christicolarum induit abitum seseque
> caelicolarum adscisci numero . . . (30:1).

In fact the concatenation of the rhyming words may be reminiscent of, hence later than, and perhaps influenced by the trope.

9. We may now propose the following theses. (a) Permission in Benedict's case was to enter a particular monastic community; in William's case it was to a new life style. Note the use of the word *anastrophe* (manner of life) in the New Testament (Gal. 1:13, Eph. 4:22; I Tim. 4:12; Heb. 12:7), in every instance translated in the Vulgate by the Latin word *conversatio*. Ardo used the related word *conversio* as a synonym (21:1) and so did the Benedictine *Rule*. We may at this point add that "Christian" became in the course of time an occasional *name* for a person converted to Christianity from Islam or Judaism.[80] (b) Permission to Benedict was granted by the monastery of Saint Seine; to William it was granted either by the Frankish emperor *or by a circle to which William formerly belonged*. (c) For Benedict the tonsure was voluntary and orderly (*comam deposuit*), but for William it did not appear to be an entirely free act (*Nec mora in deponendo comam fieri passus est*; observe the passive quality of the assertion and the fact that he "suffered it to be done"). (d) Benedict's habit was the usual monastic garb. Was William's habit, that "of Christians," in this instance, therefore, baptismal?

10. I suggest that the account in chapter 30, however muted, was of an astounding event in the

Carolingian world, comparable to the opposite conversion of Bodo, a Christian court chaplain, into Eleazar, an active Jewish propagandist in Muslim Spain.[81] This assumption tends to explain Florenz of Wevelinkhofen's fourteenth century mention of William's conversion from Christianity to Judaism, then back to Christianity.[82] It is clearly in error about William's conversion to Judaism; that is probably a conflation with the Bodo-Eleazar affair. Zuckerman is right in supposing that "it hardly would have been possible for a Jewish convert from Christianity to remain at court . . . or within reach of the authorities."[83] But it is evident that *Jews as such* could do so and in fact did. They were a highly respected minority with powerful influence.[84] William as a Jew by birthright (if Zuckerman's evidence is accepted) could be and was held in lofty esteem. By turning to Christianity (perhaps, although not certainly, to monasticism), William created a furore among both Jews and Christians comparable to that raised in similar way by Bodo-Eleasar later, the vague memory of which was exploited by Florenz of Wevelinkhofen.

11. We can accept Zuckerman's comments as apt: "The conclusion appears inescapable that no authentic contemporary document reports William's assumption of the monastic habit. This is altogether a fabrication dating no earlier than the eleventh century."[85] But Zuckerman neglected his best internal evidence: he did not make anything of a very ambiguous passage in the interpolation which noted that William, although dedicating himself wholly to Christ, did not abandon any "trace of worldly ostentation" (*nichil mundanae pompae relinquens vestigium*, 30:4).[86]

12. We must now revert to the issue of William's

source of "permission to be converted." Was it from the Jewish community or from his Frankish political superiors? It is worth recalling that Bodo-Eleazar secured no permission from either source. But William was a loyal subject of the Frankish ruler. It is, of course, possible that he first discussed conversion with his Jewish confrères, but it is much more likely that as an eminent landed nobleman he required permission from his secular ruler for "any great or important undertaking," even baptism, involving as it did a change of life style. One may account for the conversion of William on prudential grounds, perhaps to insure that his property would go to his sons, perhaps in some way to protect them. It is significant that his most famous son was baptized with Louis the Pious standing as sponsor.[87]

13. Here we are led to accept two further corrections made by Zuckerman in the traditional accounts. First, his suggestion that Bernard, William's son, was born about 806 is surely appropriate.[88] I had already reached a like conclusion about fifteen years before Zuckerman's book appeared.[89] Second, his presumption that William did not die before 814, but "closer to 822,"[90] "around the reputed date of death of the monk [Benedict] of Aniane,"[91] makes for a better understanding of the material before us, although the date was anticipated several years before Zuckerman by David Knowles.[92]

THE LIFE OF BENEDICT OF ANIANE, by Ardo

Preface

(a) To the venerable masters, fathers and brothers, serving God Jesus at the monastery of Inde, Ardo,[1] slave of Messiah's servants, sends greeting.

(b) A long time ago, my beloved brothers, your letters were delivered to me, letters full of love for the pious memory of our Father Abbot Benedict. They contained briefly but livingly an account of his death and departure to Messiah. In them you deigned to suggest to my littleness[2] that I write more elaborately for those who want to hear about the beginning of his manner of life. Thus far, however, I have demurred, being aware of the burden on my abilities.

(c) If only by perceptive zeal care could be taken by those composing a life of persons who went before — a life respected for merits and famed for virtues — not to overlook profitable matters when led to do so by partiality; if they could write with fluent pen only matters scrupulously ascertained and confirmed by report of trustworthy witnesses, they would not embarrass the ears of scholars by offering the blemish of inelegance.[3] They would present words savoring of witty urbanity and with polished language titillate the ears of detractors.

(d) But conscious of my shortcomings, I have long

46

maintained silence even though persuaded to acquiesce in your request. I have refrained so that it might be expressed by more learned persons, believing that it was surely unfair for me with inept verbiage to touch the life of so great a patron. I have deferred the appropriate task to more skillful writers. With flowing supply of words they can make clear (and even with a flourish) whatever they wish, since they have nothing to fear. They can steer the vessel between the sandbanks[4] and avoid the bad odor of grammatical errors. Gifted with facility of language they have that abundance of speech which checks the tongues of detractors.

(e) I was fearful that readers, irritated at what was badly constructed, might seek to correct clumsy composition.[5] They would thus adjudge the content to be ignored, especially since I knew that you were present at the entrance to the sacred hall of the palace, that you thirsted for no drink of boisterous streams, but eagerly drained the flow of wisdom from an unfailing watercourse of the purest fountain. Such reasoning restrained me for the space of a year.

(f) In the meanwhile you brothers undertook to rouse my lethargic inclination with stinging words, you brothers whom with holy endeavor Benedict begot for Messiah. You constrained me to bring him to life for you by tales [*gestis*][6] of his life in religion. It is certain that you are absent from him only in fellowship with his bodily presence, not in fullness of charity. So I am finally about to unfold a composition. Even the place, originally erected by him, and the brothers, who knew the beginning of his way of life, have given me a bold and favorable purpose. For what to some can scarcely be unheard, can by them hardly be unseen. Since the materials have been comprehensively assembled, we are ready to disclose more elaborately those that are suitable for the task. We severely confine as it were a seedbed as we are about to publish it more widely.

(g) We humbly beg that if anyone finds this work distasteful he will leave it alone or correct it.[7] Otherwise he may allow others to read and study it while he turns himself to reading the life[8] of earlier fathers. But if he should find that this man did not stray from their path and influence, let him be glad. If he must refute it, let it not be a hasty judgment. Let him interrupt himself and refer it tearfully to the just and peaceful Judge.

(h) Since I have obeyed your request, holy brothers, I ask you to aid me by prayers to God for pardon of my faults and for future readers to make progress by reading this book.[9] I beg you to read it with watchful zeal. Correct in detail whatever you may show to be in error. If there are useful matters in it, cherish them in the secret of your breast. By removing the force of silence we have at your command provided a mood, if not an outward act. But you must attribute our speaking to yourselves, remembering that you compelled us to break silence.[10]

(i) Abbot Helisachar[11] clung to Benedict with a disposition of unique love as he left this world — so the abbot's letter, more precious than gold, addressed to us bears witness.[12] For that reason, after you have examined this book, I think it should be presented to him in particular. Should he decide for it to be suppressed, I beg forgiveness for my error.[13] But should he deem it useful, let those who freely obeyed Benedict when he was alive, now devote themselves to imitating his life although he is absent.

48

(j) Every scholar knows, I suppose, that there is a very ancient custom, still practiced by kings, for matters that are done or events that occur to be committed to annals for the information of future generations. The mind becomes blind to various happenings when forgetfulness supervenes. We therefore believe it divinely planned for things to be preserved in records so that obliging forgetfulness and scurrying time may not efface them. Those who desire to read such chronicles take pleasure in them. They are gladdened and they turn themselves to expressions of gratitude. An author of such a record is not judged rash by them even if it does not resound with polished words and even if an avid reading of it may require great exertion.

(k) Let them agree with us both to read the life of those going before us and to entrust to posterity what in our own times we have seen or heard so as to spur souls on to progress. Let us who emit the odor of crudity not be condemned for unskilled language. We deem it sufficient to draw forth a salutary patter albeit with rude words and to exhibit delicious honey in rough honeycombs. Let each one take by his own choice what he finds acceptable to his mind.

The Life of Benedict

Chapter 1:1. That venerable man, by name and merit Abbot Benedict, was sprung from the nation of the Getae [Goths] in the area of Gothia.[14] Born of noble origin he was, but heavenly religion ennobled him by even greater brilliance of character. His father held the county of Maguelonne as long as he lived. With all his might he was loyal to the nation of

Franks.[15] He was courageous and clever, and to enemies very dangerous. With vast slaughter, as everyone knows, he overthrew the Basques who entered the frontiers of the Frankish realm to lay it waste. None escaped except the one who was saved by precipitate flight. He entrusted his aforesaid son, while still in boyhood years, to the court of glorious King Pepin to be brought up amid the queen's scholars. Bearing his age with natural quality of mind, Benedict was beloved by his comrades in arms.[16] He was of nimble wit and adaptable in everything. Later he received the office of cupbearer. He performed military service in the days of the aforesaid king. After the latter's death and the accession of most glorious King Charles,[17] Benedict was attached to him in service.

1:2. In the meanwhile divine grace enlightened him. He began to blaze with heavenly love to abandon this flaming world with all its exertions[18] and to shun that perishable honor which he realized that one could attain with effort, but once gained could quickly lose. Brooding over this in his heart for a period of three years, he kept it secret except from God. He continued to associate himself in body, though not in mind, with activities of the world.[19] During that interval he tried to grasp the pinnacle of continence, to deprive his body of sleep, to check his tongue, to abstain from food, to take wine sparingly, and to prepare himself like a skilled athlete[20] for future struggle. While still in secular habit he pondered those matters he afterwards fulfilled with devotion.

1:3. Although he wanted to divest himself of activities of the world, he hesitated about the ways in which that could be done: whether to assume the habit

D

of a pilgrim, or perhaps attach himself to someone to take care of men's sheep and cattle without pay, or even to engage in the shoemaker's craft in some city and spend on poor folk whatever profit he might be able to gain. While his mind was vacillating in such debate, he turned himself to love of life under the *Rule*.

Chapter 2:1. In the year that Italy was made subject to the sway of glorious King Charles, Benedict's brother sought recklessly to ford a certain river, but he was caught up in the swelling waves. Benedict was sitting on his horse watching when he perceived his brother's peril, but he plunged headlong into the flood to rescue the drowning exile from danger. As his horse swam forward Benedict grasped his brother's hand. The brother took hold and held on desperately. He who wanted to rescue the drowning man barely escaped death.[21] Then and there Benedict bound himself by a vow to God not to serve the world any further. He returned to his home land but did not tell his father about his intention.

2:2. Now there was a certain religious named Widmar who lacked bodily sight, but in his heart shone with light. To him Benedict revealed his desire. Widmar kept the secret and offered salutary counsel. When everything was ready, Benedict undertook a journey as though to go to Aix. But when he reached the house of Saint Seine, he ordered his companions to return to their native country, then announced that he wanted to serve Messiah God in that monastery. He thereupon requested permission to enter. When that was obtained, he soon laid aside the hair of his head and put on the habit of a true monk.

2:3. When Benedict became a monk he proceeded

to damage his body with incredible fasting for the space of two years and six months.[22] In that way he was, of course, endangering his own flesh as if it were a bloodthirsty beast. He took scanty food, sustaining his body with bread and water to avert death but not hunger, shunning wine as if it were a noxious poison. When his mind was overpowered and he sought a little sleep, he would rest for a short while by lying down on a cheap quilt.[23] Sometimes prostrate on the bare ground, he rested when excessively exhausted, but only in order to fatigue himself even more by such rest.[24] Often spending the whole night in prayer he kept himself awake by standing with bare feet on the pavement in the icy cold. He devoted himself so completely to divine meditation that he would continue many days in sacred Psalms without breaking the rule of silence.

2:4. While others were asleep he cleaned their shoes with water and oiled them, then returned them to their proper places.[25] Certain ones, alas, like jeering madmen, threw their boots at him as he stood some distance away. Their insane foolishness he endured with lofty serenity and high purpose. In his own clothing he reduced himself with such disregard that it was scarcely possible for those, who did not know better, to be persuaded that it was as it appeared. He had a cheap old tunic that he did not change until many days had elapsed.[26] Inevitably a colony of lice grew on his filthy skin, feeding on his limbs emaciated by fasts. His cowls were threadbare with extreme age. When the old threads were finally broken, he patched the rent with any available rag even if of a different color, a fact that rendered him somewhat unsightly.[27] He was, therefore, ridiculed, shoved, spat upon by many people,[28] but his mind, fixed upon heaven, sought even cheaper materials. On festal days, when others put on neater clothes, he wore his old ones without any timidity. During that period he never indulged his body in baths. Yet he employed himself for the cleanliness of the monastery as often as opportunity demanded.

2:5. The grace of compunction[29] and divine help were granted to him in such large measure that he could weep at will. In fear of Gehenna[30] he was daily sustained by tears and groans as he sang lovingly the Davidic words, "I mix ashes for bread to be eaten and my cup with tears" [Ps. 102:10].[31] His face grew gaunt with fasting; his flesh was exhausted by privation; his shriveled skin hung from his bones like the dewlaps of cows. Not so much taming a young but ungovernable animal, as mortifying the body, he was compelled by the abbot to exercise rigor against himself more sparingly. But he did not in any way express agreement. Declaring that the *Rule* of blessed Benedict was for beginners and weak persons, he strove to climb up to the precepts of blessed Basil and the rule of blessed Pachomius.[32] However much the Benedictine *Rule* might regulate possible things for paltry people, our Benedict perennially explored more impossible things. Dedicating himself wholly to penance and lamentation, he could not be imitated by anyone or only by a few. But divine favor decreed that he would become an example of salvation for many. He was inflamed with love of the *Rule* of Benedict, and like a new athlete[33] just back from single combat he entered the field to fight publicly. In the meanwhile he undertook to correct the manners of some, to scold the negligent, exhort beginners, admonish the upright to persevere, and upbraid the wicked to turn from their ways.

2:6. After that it was enjoined upon him to supervise the cellar. There he committed to memory the *Rule* of the aforesaid Father Benedict. According to its regulations he sought with all his might to establish himself firmly, then without delay to be generous to those seeking lawful things, to deny those seeking in a bad way, and courteously to make excuse for those inquiring for impossible things. Because he did not freely provide them cups, he was not regarded with favor by many. The care of guests, children, and poor folk he exercised with assiduity.[34] Moreover the abbot esteemed him with supreme fondness, because he was beneficial in everything, circumspect in his own life, solicitous for the salvation of others, prompt in ministering, infrequent in speaking, ready to obey, good-natured in serving. Divine pity conferred on him, among other virtues, the gift of understanding and a supply of spiritual eloquence.

Chapter 3:1. The space of five years and eight months[35] having flown by in salutary manner, the abbot of that monastery departed from the world. With one mind and joint agreement all chose Benedict to be set over them. But knowing that there was no compatibility between their manner and his, he hurriedly set out toward his paternal soil. There, on property belonging to his father and himself, at the brook called Aniane near the river Saône, he along with Widmar and a few others erected for their residence a small hut close to the modest church of Saint Saturninus. For several years he lived there in great poverty. For nights and days he entreated divine clemency with groanings and tears for his desire to effect powerful fruition. At the same time in that province there were certain active men of great holiness, namely, Atilio, Nibridius, and Anianus,[36] living a religious life, but unaware of supervision by the *Rule*. When Benedict became known to them, they held him in high esteem. When adverse influence tried to overcome him, he would saddle his little donkey quickly and hurry away to Atilio, his nearest neighbor.

3:2. At first many who abandoned the world attempted to live the religious life with him. But weak in spirit and afraid of a new manner of life when compelled to embrace an unheard of way of abstinence, such as receiving bread by weight and wine by measure, they soon retraced their steps which they once set on the road to salvation, and returned like swine to mire and a dog to his vomit [cf. II Pet. 2:22]. The man of God observed their unsteady faith and being disturbed decided to go back to his own monastery.

3:3. For that reason Benedict approached Atilio for counsel. When he related his wish, Atilio scolded him, "It has been revealed to me from heaven that you are given to men as a lamp [cf. Acts 13:47]. It would be fitting for you to complete the good work [cf. Phil. 1:6] you have begun. This trouble has come to pass by deceit of the ancient enemy who always grudges, always hates good deeds. No concession should ever be made to him." Bolstered by Atilio's advice, Benedict fearlessly applied himself with ardent spirit to what he longed to accomplish. Not building upon another's foundation [Rom. 15:20], he began with new endeavor to erect houses as well as to expound the strange new way [cf. Acts 17:19f.] of salvation.

Chapter 4:1. A few brothers assembled about him,

indeed flocked to him, when his belief became known; and the venerable Benedict began to flourish in holy religion at that place. He was free to expound the heavenly road to those who wanted it and to labor with his own hands. Lest as he preached to others he should be found dishonest, he took care to fulfill what Atilio had warned him should be pursued. For he did not through fear of want give up the work he had begun. On the contrary, as the Apostle says, beset by hunger and thirst, in cold and nakedness [II Cor. 11:27], he urged his subordinates to persist with untroubled heart, teaching that the way that leads to life is constricted and narrow [cf. Matt. 7:14], that the sufferings of this time are not comparable to future glory that will be revealed to the holy ones [cf. Rom. 8:18]. Strengthened by his example, his students yearned to be exhausted by even heavier labors.

4:2. At that time they had no possessions, no vineyards, no cattle, no horses. There was only one small donkey. By its help the weariness of the brothers was relieved when it was necessary for them in turn to travel any distance. They received wine only on Lord's days and festivals. Their hunger was occasionally assuaged with milk brought by neighboring women. They wasted their bodies by dehydration, living only on bread and water. To ward off the constant cold, they used blankets when they attended divine vigils. They were indeed poor in possessions, but wealthy in merits. The more their bodies were impaired with want, the more their souls were fattened with virtues. They glowed with heavenly love; tears alone brought them consolation in their poverty. The ancient foe, observing their unconquered brotherly unity [cf. Ps. 133:1], strove to divide it by craft.

4:3. They had only one mill nearby in which they ground what provisions they might have. One night a visitor, goaded by mean thoughts, came to them. They made him as comfortable as possible in the donkey's stall. But, watching with evil intent, he got up as soon as they were asleep and left, taking along what he lay on, the jug from which he drank water, and even the tools of the mill, thus repaying evil for good [cf. I Thess. 5:15]. The next morning the students reported to the master the loss they had discovered. He taught them to endure with good will injuries inflicted on them and to consider losses as gain [cf. Phil. 3:7f.], protesting to them rather to grieve for him who forgot faith while straining to take advantage.

Chapter 5:1. In the meanwhile the band of students began gradually to increase. The fame of holy religion began by degrees to flit by the mouths of those dwelling nearby,[37] spreading itself to places a long distance away. Because the valley in which he had made his first residence was very narrow, he undertook little by little to erect by new effort a monastery beyond its confines. Sometimes he labored with the brothers as they worked; sometimes he had his hands full with cooking food for them to eat, while at the same time he was also occupied even in the kitchen with writing a book. Often because of scarcity of oxen he carried wood on his own shoulders along with his students.

5:2. There was a building on the place where they were endeavoring to establish the monastery which they expanded and dedicated in honor of Holy Mary Mother of God. Since they were flocking thither from everywhere, begging zealously to submit themselves to his superintendency, the fabric of the monastery was quickly completed. The place was endowed and increased with properties as various persons offered what they had. Benedict had given order not to cover or make the houses with ornate walls, red roof tiles, or painted panelings, but with thatch and cheap timber. Although the number of brothers was rapidly expanding, he still strove for cheaper and more modest materials.

5:3. If anyone wanted to bestow some of his possessions on the monastery, Benedict took it. But if a person pressed to attach serving men and women to it, he refused. He moreover permitted no one to be delivered to the monastery by charter, but ordered them to be set free. For himself he preferred that vessels for Messiah's body not be of silver. To him first choice was wooden vessels, secondly glass, and finally tin. He refused to have a silken chasuble. If some person gave him one, he immediately gave it away to others.

Chapter 6. In the mean time in the same region or thereabout some religious men constructed monasteries and assembled monks, disciplining themselves according to the blessed man's example. Steeped in his instruction, they pruned away their former life and old errors. To them he was like a father, bringing assistance and support not only in spiritual matters, but also in material. Often visiting them he urged them not to abandon the work they had begun lest the spirit, oppressed by want and worn by terrors, might look backwards. And so monasteries, sustained by wholesome testimony, became numerous and the multitude of monks was at a peak.

Chapter 7:1. At the same time a severe famine occurred.[38] Many poor folk, widows, and orphans began to pour upon him and to fill the gates and roads of the monastery. When he saw them languishing for lack of nourishment, almost swallowed up by death itself, he was troubled because he did not know how he could feed such a number [cf. John 6:5]. But since nothing is lacking to those who fear God [cf. Job 8:12], whatever new fruits they might lay hands on to suffice the brothers he ordered to be set aside separately. He then gave command to distribute the rest through brothers designated for each day. Meat of cattle and sheep was given out every day and even goat's milk provided sustenance. They made huts for themselves in suitable places where they could dwell until the new harvests.

7:2. When food began to fail, Benedict gave another order to measure out what he had commanded to be set aside for the brothers' use. That was done three times. Among the brothers the mood of pity was so strong that they would have weighed out everything if it had been permitted. What each one was entitled to withdraw for himself, he secretly allotted to those consumed with hunger. Even so they were barely rescued from the peril of famine, for several times a man was found dead although there was bread in his mouth.

Chapter 8:1. I do not think one should maintain silence when at the same time the baneful doctrine of Felicianism invaded that province.[39] Unharmed by the noxious error of unbelief, Benedict avoided it inwardly by divine help and by his zeal rescued not only the lowliest, but also prelates of the church. Armed with javelins of debate he often joined battle against the infamous doctrine.

8:2. There was at that time also a band of brothers already numerous and inflamed with ardor for eternal life. They vied indeed who of them might be humbler, who prompter in obedience, who more zealous in abstinence, who more forward in vigils, who slower to speak, who cheaper in dress, and who more fervent in charity. Revelations were also made to certain ones.

Chapter 9. There was a certain brother who was by no means disposed to human honor. When Father Benedict noticed that he was making his way apparently negligently, he concluded the same rudeness in his spirit. But caught up in an ecstasy the man saw a flock of doves, some gleaming with marvelous whiteness, some distinguished by an amazing variety of colors, some marked with a repulsive color on the head. Soon he realized what this meant and the names of each were spoken: negligence made some black, zeal made some gleam brightly. Returning to himself [cf. Luke 15:17], he related to Father Benedict what he had seen and warned him not to despise him. Searching the deeds of each, Benedict then discovered the minds of the brothers distraught just as he learned from the ecstatic and therefore restored them to suitable pattern by imposing a kindly emollient of reproof.

Chapter 10. The ancient foe tolerated with difficulty the unity and increase of the good flock. He tried to agitate the hearts of certain ones to make the good founder an exile from his own sheepfold. By his craft he drove many away from the monastery and unsettled others. Although he could not dismay the mind prepared for tribulation, he nursed back to life latent forces that were broken and about to perish, by inciting them to take away horses and cattle both secretly and openly. But he who has set God before everything loses without grief what he possessed without love.

Certainly no one ever saw Benedict upset over anything that was lost; he never sought to recover what was destroyed; he never looked for what was stolen. If a thief was caught, Benedict offered kindness and quietly released him so he would not be caught again.

Chapter 11:1. A certain one who stealthily removed the monastery's horses was captured by neighbors and wounded. When he was brought before Father Benedict, the latter furnished him expenses, summoned a physician, and sent him unharmed to the infirmary.

11:2. On another occasion, when the venerable father was making a journey in company with a brother, they met a man astride a horse stolen from the monastery. The brother stared inquiringly and recognized it as one that had been stolen. He immediately blurted out that it was the monastery's horse. But Benedict told him to keep quiet, "One horse is often similar to another." Aside he remonstrated with the brother, "I, too, recognized it, but I think it is better to remain silent than to create a sense of embarrassment."

Chapter 12:1. Since almighty God, who created all things, performs on suitable occasions miracles through His servants, I will compress into a brief narrative some that He wrought through Benedict.

12:2. [First miracle story] Once upon a time a fire broke out in a house located near the basilica of the Blessed Virgin Mary. When the devouring flame licked at the dry thatch, the grieving brothers ran thither. They watched the house they had built with great labor as it was being consumed by the leaping flames. They busied themselves with earnest zeal to prevent the fire from spreading to the neighboring church, for the whole fury of the flame was tending in that direction. Father Benedict approached the spectacle. At once the brothers importuned him to help them with his prayers. Quickly complying with the brothers' urgency, he threw himself with tears before the altar of the Blessed Virgin Mary Mother of God. While he was praying, the fury of the fire suddenly turned with the aid of divine mercy in another direction.[40]

Chapter 13. [Second miracle] At the same time, too, there was a great flight of locusts that hid the sun's rays with its thickness.[41] They settled in massed attack on the vineyard that lay near the monastery to devastate it. The brothers were accustomed to receive their cups chiefly from it. The venerable man entered the basilica of the Blessed Mother of God and with tear-drenched face and voice implored divine aid. After a little while the locusts became restless and left.

Chapter 14. [Third miracle] By another chance fire attacked a neighboring mountain, licking at the dry straw, the branches, and the earth parched by the sun's heat. Moved by its own impetus, it threatened ruin to the vineyard and monastery. To extinguish it all the brothers gathered. With them came venerable Father Benedict. Suddenly the fire abandoned the path it had begun and quickly subsided on right and left. Except for Benedict's prayers, I think, it must be supposed that conflagration would have prevailed.

Chapter 15. [Fourth miracle] A certain brother was enjoined to guard the cattle. As he left the monastery to go to his duty, he sought Father Benedict for a blessing. "May the Lord protect you," said the latter as he bestowed the sign of the cross. When the brother reached the pasture, he encountered bandits in this manner. Approaching without any suspicion, he was halted by them. They seized the reins of the horse on which he was sitting. After peering at him a long time in silence, they let him go — and he left in a hurry. When he told the father, the latter remarked, "God's blessing did preserve you unharmed."

Chapter 16. What I have personally seen should not be passed over in silence. A certain brother was made provost. Falling into pride, he was deposed from his office. At length he became so spiteful that he decided to leave the monastery and practice robbery. Thus it was that he decided to steal a horse surreptitiously from the monastery itself. When he tried to do so, Benedict commanded him to be driven away with his feet tied under the horse. But he began to bawl and swear that he would never depart from the monastery. Because of his folly, Benedict gave order to beat him lightly with switches. Thereafter he remained in the monastery, living properly and piously, as if he himself were the smitten malign foe.

Chapter 17:1. Thus far what is said may suffice concerning the life of so great a father as, by the light of divine clemency, he abandoned the world and removed to the regions of Gothia to erect by new endeavor a monastery. Now by Messiah's aid we may unfold with clearness how by Charles's command he constructed another monastery in the same place.

17:2. In the year 782, the fourteenth of King Charles the Great, Benedict, with dukes and counts aiding him, undertook to construct another large church in honor of our Lord and Savior, but differently. He no longer covered the houses with thatch but with tiles and adorned the cloisters with as many marble columns as possible placed in the porches. The place was furnished by them with such holiness that whoever might seek in faith would come not doubting in his heart, but believing [cf. James 1:6] that what he might need would come to pass.

17:3. Because it glistened with outstanding religious observance, we deem it appropriate to relate for future generations some things about the location of that place. Venerable Father Benedict decided upon pious reflection to consecrate the aforesaid church not by the title of one of the saints but in the name of the Holy Trinity. For it to be more clearly recognized, he determined that three small altars should be placed near the main altar so that by them the persons of the Trinity may be figuratively indicated. A marvelous arrangement it is: by the three altars the undivided Trinity is shown forth and by the single altar the true Godhead in essence is shown forth. The great altar is one solid surface on the front, but inwardly concave. In figure it suggests what Moses built in the desert. It has a little door behind where on ferial [i.e., ordinary] days chests containing various relics of the fathers are enclosed. The foregoing statements suffice concerning the altar.

17:4. We now pass briefly to the furnishing of the building, in what order or number it is arranged. All the vessels that are kept in the building are consecrated to the number seven. For instance, there are seven candelabra curiously wrought by the craftsman's art. From the arms project branches, little spheres, with lilies, reeds, and bowls, after the manner of a nut tree, done like that which Bezaleel contrived with his wonderful skill [cf. Ex. 37:17-22; 36:1]. In front of the altar hang seven lamps, marvelous and beautiful, spread with incredible effort, lighted in the manner of Solomon by trained persons eager to tend them [cf. II Chron. 8:14 and Ex. 30:7].

17:5. In the same way other lamps, silver ones, hang in the choir in the form of a crown with containers inserted in circles. It was customary on special feasts to fill them with oil and light them. When they were lighted the whole church was aglow at night as if it were day. Lastly three further altars in the basilica were dedicated, one in honor of Saint Michael the archangel, another in devotion to the blessed Apostles Peter and Paul, and a third in honor of good Stephen the protomartyr.

17:6. In the church of Blessed Mary Mother of God which was first established, there are altars of Saint Martin and blessed Benedict. But that one which is built in the cemetery is distinguished in honor of Saint John the baptizer, than whom among those born of women none greater has arisen, as the divine oracles testify [cf.Matt. 11:1].[42] It is appropriate to ponder with what profound humility and reverence this place was feared by them, this place protected by so many princes. The Lord Messiah is indeed the Prince of all princes, King of kings, and Lord of lords. Blessed Mary Mother of God is held to be queen of all virgins. Michael is placed over all angels. Peter and Paul are chiefs of the apostles. Stephen the protomartyr holds first place in the choir of witnesses. Martin shines as a gem of prelates. Benedict is father of all monks. By the seven altars, by the seven candelabra, and by the seven lamps, the sevenfold grace of the Holy Spirit is understood [cf. Isa. 11:2f.].

Chapter 18:1. Whoever he is who seeks to read or listen to this biography, let him realize that Aniane is the head of all monasteries, not only of those erected in the regions of Gothia, but also of those erected in other areas at that time or afterwards according to the example of this one and enriched with the treasures of Benedict, as this document will hereinafter relate. He gave his heart to studying the *Rule* of blessed Benedict. To be able fully to understand it, he visited various monasteries and inquired of any skilled persons what he did not know. He assembled the rules of all the holy ones as he was successful in discovering them. He taught a useful standard and wholesome custom for monasteries which he transmitted to his own monks to be observed. He established cantors, taught lectors, secured grammarians, and scholars in Scriptural knowledge. From them certain ones became bishops.[43] He collected a multitude of books, assembled costly vestments, large silver chalices, and silver offertory vessels.

18:2. Whatever he observed as needful for Divine Office he obtained with enthusiasm. He became known to everyone and the fame of his sanctity reached the ears of the emperor. Later he went to most glorious Emperor Charles for the benefit of the monastery. Moved by pious consideration, Charles granted the monastery to Benedict by charter, so that after the emperor's death the witnesses would not permit any disruptions by his successors. From Charles Benedict soon received an 'immunity' containing the following:

18:3. "In the name of the holy and undivided Trinity, Charles, by God's grace king of the Franks and Lombards and patrician of the Romans.[44] We believe that fortification of our realm will reach its greatest peak if, with well-wishing devotion, we concede suitable locations as benefits for churches. With the Lord's protection we decree them to endure without variations. Be it therefore known to all

E

bishops, abbots, counts, viscounts, vicars, hundred-men, judges, and all the faithful, present and future alike, how the venerable man, Abbot Benedict, came to our clemency from the monastery he himself built up by new effort and by his own right from the foundations in honor of our Lord and Savior, Jesus the Messiah, of the holy and ever-virgin Mary Mother of God, and of other saints, in the place called Aniane, in the countryside of Maguelonne, near the fortress of Montcalm. With complete purpose he assigned to our hands the aforesaid monastery with all properties and ornaments of the church, whether attached to it or adjacent, and committed that holy place to us to rule with our protection and government.

18:4. "At his special petition, therefore, we have granted for the sake of eternal reward a benefit to that holy place in this manner. In respect of churches, places, fields, or other properties of that monastery, which it rightly has in modern times by our gift and confirmation or that of other faithful ones, in whatever locations, whatever has been conferred there for the sake of divine love, whatever else holy religion may hereafter add in the right of that holy place, whether by us or others, we command them to receive. Moreover we pronounce a curse to the effect that no count, bishop, or any judicial authority dare at any time ever to enter or presume to force cases to be heard, taxes to be levied, habitations or provisions to be seized, sponsors to be taken away, people of that monastery, free or servants, who live on its lands to be removed, any cancelled sales or unlawful pretexts to be sought, or any property to be questioned.

18:5. "The abbot himself, his successors, and the monks, present or future, may rule the aforesaid place for the sake of God's name under complete immunity without disturbance or opposition by anyone whatever; and they may never dare for any reason to divert its property to anyone. We desire to confirm that holy place under our defense and government. We therefore declare and order that neither you nor your juniors or successors, or anyone with judicial authority shall ever, at any time, dare make disturbances or exactions in the churches, places, fields, or other possessions of the monastery aforesaid or indeed make changes in any of the matters written above; but what for the sake of the Lord's name and of eternal reward we have granted to the aforementioned monastery, may it increase and progress.

18:6. "When, at the divine summons, the venerable Abbot Benedict mentioned above or his successors depart from this life to the Lord, that holy congregation wishes to choose an abbot from the monastery described above or from whatever place, an abbot of similar kind or better, one faithful to us in all matters, one able to govern that holy congregation according to Saint Benedict's *Rule*, they have permission to do so by this our authority and indulgence. Wherever they and their monks may wish to be regulated or by whatever prelate, they have authority by our precept and consent, so long as those servants of God belonging to God's household in that place may be pleased to pray constantly for the Lord's mercy upon us, upon our wife and children; and for the stability of the entire realm committed and spared to us by God."

Chapter 19:1. Most glorious King Charles conferred that by precept upon the venerable man Benedict,[45] but the latter also received from all directions through the imperial charter useful cattle and lands suitable for farming. Dowered by the emperor with great honor, that is, almost forty pounds of silver, he returned in peace to his monastery as quickly as possible. As soon as he reached his native sod, he dispatched the silver he bore, divided for the sake of blessing, to the several monasteries. In our times he had this singular gift beyond all others, namely, a kindly and pious respect for everyone and care for all the monasteries whether near at hand or at a distance. He visited them frequently and imbued them with the regulations of holy living.

19:2. Of those materials brought to him by the faithful, he transferred according to the number of inhabitants and according to their ability, more to those in greater want, less to those requiring little. For he knew monasteries of both kinds and he remembered their names. Since he could not distribute mantles to each one, he sent them divided and made into crosses. For of all the monasteries situated as well in Provence as in Gothia and the province of Novempalitana [Gascony], he was like a nurse cherishing and aiding. He was beloved by all as father, venerated as master, and revered as teacher.

19:3. A portion for the poor was separated with greatest enthusiasm and he did not allow widows' shares to be expended for other purposes. He knew of course the names of all the nuns and widows located roundabout. Ransom was joyfully provided for captives. No one departing left him without a gift and as far as possible everything was done for everyone. For that reason each person voluntarily brought provisions to him to be laid up for distribution to the poor, needy, widows, captives, and monks. From some people he might receive as much as four or five thousand *solidi* in vessels to be apportioned among those in want.

19:4. Benedict had great concern not only to refresh his own people with food of preaching, but also to nourish with heavenly bread whomever he happened to encounter. That they might not lose the salutary food through forgetfulness, he was accustomed to impress upon them to cling tenaciously to it in their heart. This he did with such words as, "Let it be," he said, "with chaste body and humble heart, because proud chastity and vain humility are not acceptable to God." On some he was in the habit of stressing this, "If most precepts are impossible for you to remember, keep at least this short one, 'Turn away from evil and do good' [Ps. 37:27]." That sentence was so habitual to him that near the time of his death, when he had assembled statements from all the fathers, he proposed to produce one book about it alone. At every hour, whether at Nocturns, in chapter, or in refectory, he provided the food of life for all those subject to him.

Chapter 20. While we have tried to unfold his good will, a number of his virtues stand out in plain view. We will, therefore, detail a small selection of them suitable for men who do not know about them, but desire the information. Everyone attached to his 'family' knows this — that he surpassed all in charity. Never did he do anything for himself, but rather what he deemed beneficial to others. If he did otherwise, he quickly made reparation. Out of devotion to charity and in order to secure the salvation of many, he visited the cells of others and explained the obscurities of the holy *Rule*. Full of charity he spent days in Arles with many bishops, abbots, and monks,[46] explaining the mysteries of the canons and expounding the homilies of blessed Pope Gregory to ignorant ones. Filled with charity he nurtured within his own monastery clergy and monks from different localities. Appointing a teacher for them, he saturated them with sacred interpretations. In charity he sent gifts to those who did injury to him. But we should not belabor that what everyone saw better, many experienced with complaisance.

Chapter 21:1. Benedict turned away [*declinarat*][47] little by little from the rigor of his first way of life, for he had undertaken an impossible task, yet the same will remained. He plowed with plowmen, accompanied diggers, reaped with reapers. Although that region was scorched by the sun's heat, a heat as though of fire from a furnace, burning rather than heating, he rarely allowed his men, even when suffering from excessive heat, a cup of water before the hour of refreshment. Worn with labor, scorched by the heat, they desired cold water rather than wine. But no one grumbled against him, because he experienced the same. That fact brought them no little solace, for he acted more leniently toward them when he observed himself burning with thirst. Nor did any laborers dare to make noise by talking; their hands were occupied with work and their tongues with Psalms. The mouths of those going to and returning from labor were attentive to divine meditations.

21:2. We, who tried to treat him more humanely in drink and food, often saw him giving away raisins [dates].[48] We also saw him measure the dish set before him. Those who were in charge of the cellar related that he usually drank water while others were drinking wine, except on the Sabbath and the Lord's Day.[49] We had to separate any fat from his food and special care was taken lest even a small particle of common cheese be found in it. From the day of his conversion to the end of his life he chose not to eat the flesh of four-footed animals. If any illness assailed him, he took a broth made from a chicken.

21:3. For many years in his earlier day he avoided fat, yet he provided for others what he denied himself as often as there was opportunity. So great was his solicitude that if a tiny grain of vegetables, small fragment of chicken, or leaves of cabbages were overlooked by anyone, a suitable discipline was meted out for him whose fault it was proven to be. If anyone drew water for washing and poured more than was necessary (as did happen), he had to acknowledge that he had sinned by not walking the road of discernment.

21:4. Benedict possessed an unusual gift: as soon as anyone with disturbed thoughts in his mind approached him, the tumultuous crowd of thoughts dissipated at his wholesome counsel. Often indeed when a person was bombarded by unsafe thoughts (so I learned from a true brother), he would say to himself, "I will go and reveal you to Lord Benedict." At that very moment the unsuitable confusion left him. If anyone was hindered by severer faults, he received soothing consolation when he opened up his heart to Benedict. If one was oppressed by the disease of melancholy, he soon departed in happiness after visiting Benedict.[50]

Chapter 22. The throng of monks engaged in God's service increased so that there were more than three hundred. Because of so large a congregation, Benedict gave order to erect a bigger house to hold a thousand or more men. It was a hundred cubits in length and twenty in width. Moreover, because other places could not hold them, he constructed cells at convenient locations where he placed brothers with teachers to direct them.

Chapter 23. [Fifth miracle] About that time a rainstorm occurred while the brothers and their teacher were resting. Suddenly water rushed in from both doors and threatened to fill the house. The frightened brothers got up in a hurry. Latrines had been built with great effort over flowing water which began to rise and endanger them. The rivulets below began to surge with a roar and leaped up in waves at that moment to ruin the structure. Although it was nearly midnight the monks ran to the church. The father himself had already arrived there. He seized the bell rope and shouted to them to sing Lauds, to implore the suffrages of the saints, and to entreat God's mercy with tears. After much prayer they went out to see whether the building was overthrown. As the venerable man was going, night was so dark and gloomy that he ran into a bramble bush and hurt his legs. But he did not cease tearfully to beg God for the flood to abate. When they reached the location, the water was found to have subsided a whole foot. Relying on God's help they returned to their companions in the church. When they had related God's kindness, they blessed God together.

Chapter 24:1. In the mean time some bishops who heard reports of Benedict's sanctity and the holy reputation of his flock, began to demand some monks from him to serve as examples. Among them Leidrad, bishop of Lyons, wanting to rebuild the monastery of Ile-Barbe, sought with persistence those who might display for him the beginning of the good life. Benedict thereupon selected about twenty students from his flock, set a director over them, and instructed them to take up residence in the region of Burgundy.

With the Lord's assistance there has now been assembled in that area a large band of monks, thriving and flourishing in holy religion.

24:2. Theodulf, bishop of Orléans,[51] wanted to erect the monastery of Saint Maximin and demanded of Benedict some experts in the discipline of the *Rule*. The latter quickly gave assent and dispatched to him twice ten monks[52] with a teacher set over them. Since they continually vied in holy zeal, they added to themselves no small band of monks.

24:3. [Sixth miracle] I will relate what occurred there when the venerable father approached them for a visit. Awaiting his arrival, they devoted their energy to procure an abundant supply of fish and foods not only out of love for him, but also for all the brothers. There was a meeting of the brothers; fishermen were dispatched; markets were searched; but the activity eventuated in difficulty. Nothing could be found for purchase; the fish would not bite. They were filled with great sorrow because of this barren result. In the meanwhile the master arrived. They received him joyously and he, rejoicing in their progress, greeted them in return. The brothers concealed their chagrin under cheerful countenances.

24:4. In the meanwhile a certain brother was diligently pursuing his effort beside the Loire river. Suddenly he spied a large fish, one they call a salmon, swimming near the bank. The brother made no delay in springing to catch it and bring it to the others. There was joy over this, but there was even more wonderment, for they all professed that this came about owing to the merits of venerable Benedict. Unless I am in error, I learned this from a faithful brother.

24:5. Alcuin, of the Angle nation, a deacon in holy

order, venerable by merit of holiness, governing the monastery of blessed Martin (who had been bishop of Tours), was held worthy of all honor at the court of glorious Emperor Charles. When Alcuin heard and experienced the holiness of God's man, he joined himself to him in lasting charity. From his letters addressed to Benedict, a booklet has been compiled.[53] When gifts had been offered, Alcuin resolutely demanded that some monks be given to him. The venerable father at once complied and Alcuin dispatched horses to fetch them. He located them in a monastery named Cormery which he had erected. There were, I think, twenty with a teacher set over them. By their good example of life a great multitude of monks was assembled.

Chapter 25:1. I do not think it amiss if miracles done by divine grace at this time are inserted in this treatise.

25:2. [Seventh miracle] A certain brother was sent to carry from one cell to another a consecrated container in which relics of Saint Denis and other saints were put. With him he took along also some puppies, but returning after several days he negligently strove to bring back the consecrated container without having washed his clothes. He embarked hurriedly in a boat — for his cell was situated between a lake and the sea. As soon as he reached land he mounted a horse, settling the puppies first and then picking up the container to attach it. But divine punishment overthrew him: at that very moment the horse reeled in a circular motion so that the brother fell to the ground. The container slipped from his hands (it was later recovered unharmed); the horse died at once; and the brother who had fallen was knocked into unconsciousness. He remained that way a long time, but ultimately regained his health.

25:3. When the brothers learned what had happened, they sent back another brother to look for the relics. Being a priest he took along a cross in which some of the Lord's wood was embedded. As he entered the lake his boat was shaken by a mighty wind. But when he held up the cross, which he wore about his neck, to the swelling waves, the winds subsided.[54] Earlier, while he was resting in his cell, he had seen in a dream a man of dazzling brightness who addressed him thus, "Unless you take with you the Lord's wood, you will never leave here at the time you want to leave." He was also warned to carry the relics on foot. But he did not obey and, when he recovered and returned them, he was stricken with severe illness. Afterwards to the church from which the relics were removed he presented a lamp, in the vessels of which there was very little oil. But on the next day they were found to be filled. That happened three times. I learned this story from the brother who fell and fainted.

Chapter 26. [Eighth miracle] In the mountains where the brothers lived when they took care of feeding the sheep, they erected a small oratory for prayer. After the brothers departed from that place, some women entered it. Jeering at the residence of the monks, they said to one another, "You take the abbot's position and stand in his place." But as each one, who took turn in the prayer stall as though praying, knelt down, she had difficulty in rising. Those dwellings in which the monks lived remained vacant only during summer time. Suitable punishment overtook the women at once. They began to be wracked with jerks and twists.[55] They were not rescued from the pain until their husbands followed the monks as they went down the mountain with the sheep and begged them to offer prayers for the rash women. As the brothers prayed, the women were instantly restored to health.

Chapter 27:1. [Ninth miracle] A certain man from some place came to the monastery with his parents leading him. He was placed in the basilica of Blessed Mary ever Virgin Mother of God. When the brothers poured out prayers for him with vigils, his health returned and he left in peace.

27:2. [Tenth miracle] A woman filled with an unclean spirit came to the monastery. The brothers guarded her with vigils and prayers in the oratory of Saint John the baptizer, which is located at the cemetery. With God's help she, too, left in safe condition.

Chapter 28:1. [Eleventh miracle] To the oratory dedicated in honor of Saint Saturninus the martyr, where venerable Benedict first lived, to it if anyone with fever went and slept a little while, he would return in sound condition to his own estates, if he did not waver in confidence.

28:2. Let it suffice to have said these few things about miracles done in our times. With God's aid let us return to the sequence we began.[56]

Chapter 29. Most glorious Louis, then king of Aquitaine, but now by God's provident grace august emperor of the whole church in Europe,[57] discovered Benedict's way of holiness, loved him beyond measure, and freely obeyed his counsel. The emperor set him over all the monasteries in the realm[58] to exhibit to all a wholesome standard. For there were certain monasteries observing canonical institutes, but unaware of the precepts of the *Rule*. Obeying Louis's commands, Benedict traveled around the monasteries of each kind not once or twice only, but many times, showing the admonitions of the *Rule* and discussing it with them chapter by chapter, confirming what was known, revealing what was unknown. By God's foresight it therefore came to pass that almost all the monasteries located in Aquitaine accepted the plan of the *Rule*.

29:2. But he who hates good deeds, the opponent of innocence and enemy of peace, deemed it unfair not to inflict damage if Benedict persisted a long time in the pious king's friendship, if their love remained undivided. Since the devil lost the glory of his nature by pride, he is on guard with all his prowess lest a human be introduced into those good things that he lost. He takes offense that a human can be recovered by God's pity. It is no wonder that the ancient foe is tortured by the uprightness of pious persons and that he persecutes those whom he observes to be invincible in their progress. Nonetheless there are many who emulate Satan's wicked works. Although it is to be deeply lamented, many burn with alien practices; they are armed with hatred of those who choose not to follow their example.

29:3. When the aforesaid deeds were recognized as outstanding and meritorious to God, Satan, overwhelmed by their number, armed with weapons of envy, set forth to fight them with evil. First he fired the spirits of the clergy to minimize them. Then he invaded the hearts of knights of the royal court. He subverted the minds of certain counts. All equally inflamed with the faggot of envy, not secretly but openly vomiting the venom of a pestilent mind, they clamored loudly that he who always prayed for their souls was a 'wandering monk' (*circilli-onem*), greedy for property, an invader of other people's estates. Their mad fury exploded to such enormity that they tried to arouse the most serene Emperor Charles against Benedict.

29:4. But God's man with sure conscience was neither dismayed by the detractions nor frightened by false declarations. He therefore approached the palace because of that matter. As he entered no one tried to prevent him, because it was supposed that if he appeared in the emperor's presence he would not be allowed to return to his home land, since imperial anger would be aroused against him. He went in, however, without trepidation, relying on God's pity and putting his hope in Him for love of whom he strove without reluctance. If he should be sentenced to undergo pain of exile, so be it. It would make his mind freer to serve God. If he should be removed from office, he explained that with deep yearning he had long desired that boon. But when he appeared in the emperor's presence heavenly piety inclined Charles's mind to such great peace that as soon as he saw Benedict he embraced him and with his own hand extended a cup to him. Thus he, whom envious men had said would be an exile from his own soil, returned to it with high honor. And so, with divine mercy overriding, those who tried to defame him actually praised him[59] and showed him, whom they sought to render odious by lies, not only revered by the least, but also by the greatest.

Interpolation: William of Gellone

Chapter 30:1. Count William, who was more outstanding at the emperor's court than all others,[60] clung to blessed Benedict with such fondness that he scorned the dignities of the world and chose him as his leader in that way of salvation by which he might attain to Messiah [cf. Phil. 3:8]. Permission to be converted was finally received and he bestowed on the venerable man vast amounts of gold, silver, and costly vestments. William endured no delay in allowing his hair to be shorn. On the birthday of the Apostles Peter and Paul [29 June], he laid aside clothes woven of gold and put on the habit of Christians, rejoicing that he was so quickly added to the number of heaven-dwellers.[61]

30:2. There was a valley about four miles away from blessed Benedict's monastery. It was called Gellone. There the aforesaid count, hitherto so high in the world's dignity, gave order to construct a cell wherein he committed himself to serve Messiah for the duration of his life. Although born of noble origin, he was zealous to make himself Messiah's by embracing a nobler poverty. For Messiah he rejected the highest honor he had inherited.

30:3. I think it worthwhile to relate, for those who do not know, some of the religious deeds of his manner of life. In the aforesaid cell Father Benedict had already placed his monks. Imbued with their example, within a few days William excelled in virtues those by whom he was taught. With the aid of his sons[62] whom he had set over his counties and of neighboring counts, he quickly brought to completion the fabric of the monastery he had begun. That place was so remote that he who dwelled there could not wish for solitude.

On all sides it was surrounded by cloud-covered mountains. No one had access to it but one whom a willing spirit drew there for the sake of prayer. It was bathed in such pleasantness that one could desire no other place if he decided to serve God. Vineyards were there which William ordered planted, an abundance of gardens, a valley packed with different kinds of trees. He acquired a great many possessions.

30:4. At his request, the most serene King Louis expanded it with a spacious boundary, granting from his own treasure funds to work the areas. The king gave many holy vestments, furnished silver and gold chalices and vessels for the offertory, brought along many books, clothed the altars with gold and silver. Into this cell William entered, dedicated himself wholly to Messiah, abandoning all trace of worldly ostentation.[63] He was of such profound humility that seldom if ever could a monk whom he happened to meet bow low enough not to be surpassed by him in abjection. We often saw him mount his donkey to carry flagons of wine to the barn, himself seated thereon bearing a chalice over his shoulders on his back, visiting the brothers of our monastery at harvest time to slake their thirst. He was so wakeful at vigils that he surpassed everyone. At the mill he worked with his own hands unless another occupation hindered or illness impeded him. He completed the baking in his turn. In dress he wore the standard vesture of deepest humility. He was a lover of fasting, constant in prayer, unwearying in compunction. Scarcely ever did he receive Messiah's body without streams of tears falling to earth. He greedily sought harshness of bed, but because of his poor health Father Benedict had a blanket spread beneath him although he did not want it.

30:5. Some say that for love of Messiah William often had himself flogged with whips, but no person other than the one who was present was aware of that practice. Often during the middle of the night and known only to God, he remained in the oratory that he had erected in honor of Saint Michael; although shivering with the icy cold and clad with one thin cloak, he was absorbed in prayer. For a few years he was full of these and other virtues. Then he realized that the day of death was threatening him. He ordered it to be made known in writing to almost all the monasteries in Lord Charles's realm when he had departed from this world. In this manner, bearing a supply of virtues, he left the world when Messiah summoned him. For those desiring to know, these matters are sufficient. Let us again return to the work we undertook.[64]

The Life of Benedict (resumed)

Chapter 31:1. Most pious King Louis, knowing how usual it is for evil persons to resent advancement of upright persons, associated himself more and more with Benedict in loving esteem as the venerable abbot was ridiculed more and more by madmen. The queen,[65] too, cherished him with pious disposition. Because Louis had come to know the good man, he willingly paid attention to him and very often bestowed gifts on him. When the multitude of students grew and the place where Benedict dwelled was unfruitful, the ground almost barren, and scorched with the sun's heat, Louis gave him the monastery situated in the Auvergne which Saint Menelaus, scion of royal origin, had founded and where his body lay. Thither Benedict directed twelve monks, setting over them as abbot a man of highest respect named Andoar, a man approved and worn by many toils, who had been with him from the earliest day of his conversion. As they labored and strove with holy zeal, seventy or more joined them to practice monastic life as fully as possible.

31:2. On one occasion the eminent Abbot Benedict went to that monastery to visit the brothers. While the abbot and brothers were awaiting his arrival at a particular place, it happened that Benedict entered that cell of the monastery where the church in honor of God and our Savior is located. The brothers had indeed at first made residence there, but because it was a narrow place the most serene king had soon transferred them to the monastery mentioned above. The brothers who were left behind to care for the cell were delighted when they saw Abbot Benedict approaching with some of his monks. They were embarrassed, however, because they were so poor. But where charity is, there is enough, so he who presided over the brothers ordered one of them to fetch wine. He replied that there was none in the vessel. The other brothers had left with them only two small vessels in which there was just enough wine with which they could say Mass or sip small amounts on Lord's days.

31:3. [Twelfth miracle] The master of that cell was downcast when he heard there was no wine in the vessel. But he spoke confidently, "Go and bring it to us. Those who are going ahead to meet him should drink out of respect for the father. It will not fail them." The brother went and turned the spigot — and wine came out! When he had first tried to get some and did not succeed, he had returned. But now he told them what was occurring. Those who were present glorified God and declared that it was accomplished by the merits of Lord Benedict. They drank, therefore, at will and took some with them to refresh the travelers. Lord Benedict and his monks arrived and accepted what was needful. Some of it he carried with him on his journey. Immediately thereafter the vessel again ceased to yield wine. I learned this from those very brothers who told me what they saw. There are some witnesses still living. [cf. I Cor. 15:6].

Chapter 32. [Thirteenth miracle] At another time Benedict went back to the same monastery. When he was getting ready to depart after a long sermon and holy conversation [cf. Acts 20:11], he offered a kiss of peace to the brothers. Among them a certain brother approached for the embrace. When the man of God saw him he stopped at once and for a moment refused the kiss of peace. Then, after a suitable rebuke at which we wondered, he kissed the brother. Another brother then presented himself. Benedict did the same to him. Finally after a last farewell he left the brothers. On the morning after he went away it was discovered that those two brothers had decided to desert. Then we knew why the venerable *abba*[66] was, under the Holy Spirit's revelation, slow to embrace them. Even if he did not openly betray their perverse intention, he nevertheless did upbraid their disturbed consciences with salutary words.

Chapter 33. At length the most glorious king gave Benedict another monastery, where I believe he sent twenty monks and an abbot. That monastery was situated in the region of Poitiers and dedicated in honor of Saint Savinus. While the brothers placed there sweated away diligently in holy zeal, no small band of monks were joined to them. Again Louis conferred on him another monastery located in the region of Bourges. There Benedict settled about forty monks and an abbot. Since that place was founded as an entirely new effort, he provided assistance and gave them books and vestments. While they were flourishing in the practice of holy religion, displaying a standard of holy life, and preserving unity of spirit in the bond of peace [Eph. 4:3], they assembled into Messiah's sheepfold a very large flock of monks.

Chapter 34. An illustrious nobleman, Wulfar by name, kinsman of Count William, gave them by charter a place to erect a monastery in the confines of Albi. Thither Benedict sent about twelve monks with an abbot ordained for them. Since they had enough to do to complete by new effort the fabric of the monastery they had undertaken, Benedict gave them also a great many books, provided them sacred vestments, and managed a silver chalice, offertory vessels, a cross, and everything he saw would be needful for them. As they struggled both in construction of material buildings and in edification of souls by the regulations of the holy *Rule*, they acquired a large congregation of religious brothers in the service of Messiah God.

Chapter 35:1. After the death of most serene Emperor Charles and after his son, King Louis of Aquitaine, assumed care of the empire, the latter ordered Benedict into the region of Frankland. Louis appointed Marmoutier in Alsace where Benedict located many followers of his kind of life from the monastery of Aniane. Since the aforesaid place was at such a distance from the palace that Benedict could not meet at a suitable time when he was summoned, and because he was required by the emperor for many occasions, it pleased Louis to provide him a convenient place not far from the palace where he could live with a few monks. Thus an abbot was set over the brothers at Marmoutier, while Benedict himself went with several in obedience to the emperor's wish.

35:2. There was a neighboring valley which is, I think, not more than six miles from the palace. It was pleasing in the eyes of God's man. There the emperor gave order to erect with amazing effort a monastery called Inde, the name of the valley itself and derived from the little river.[67] The emperor was present for dedication of the church and he endowed it abundantly from his own treasures. He gave it 'immunity' in a document[68] and decreed that thirty monks should dwell there in the service of God Messiah. To complete the number, the venerable *abba* commanded brothers selected from noted monasteries to come, whom he might instruct by his example to be lessons of salvation to others, until animated by divine grace, secular pomp abandoned, and seeking knightly service for the eternal King,[69] others might in time be selected from that province.

35:3. After that God's man began to wear away the palace floors and, for the profit of many, to endure troubles he had once set aside. All who suffered from injuries of others or who sought imperial opinions came to him. He received them with gladness and embraced them. At an opportune moment he brought their complaints set down in documents to the emperor. The most serene emperor, plucking at his napkin or sleeves,[70] received them, read them as he found them, and decided as usefully as he knew how after becoming acquainted with them. But sometimes he put them away and forgot them.[71] Yet the emperor willingly listened to complaints of this kind and for that reason ordered Benedict to be at the palace as unremittingly as possible.

35:4. There were many who consulted the abbot about direction of the realm, about disposition of provinces, and about their own advantage. No one in fact had such compassion on the miseries of the afflicted; no one revealed to the emperor the needs of monks as he did. Benedict was an advocate of the wretched, but a father of monks; a comforter of the poor, but a teacher of monks. He provided the food of life for rich people, but he inculcated the discipline of the *Rule* upon the minds of monks.

Chapter 36:1. The emperor therefore set Benedict over all monasteries in his realm,[72] that as he had instructed Aquitaine and Gothia in the standard of salvation, so also might he imbue Frankland with a salutary example. Many monasteries had once been established in the *Rule*, but little by little firmness had grown lax and regularity of the *Rule* had almost perished. That there might be one wholesome usage for all monasteries, as there was one profession by all, the emperor ordered the fathers of monasteries to assemble with as many monks as possible. They were in session for many days.[73] When all had come together, Benedict elucidated obscure points to all as he discussed the entire *Rule*; he made clear doubtful points; he swept away old errors; he confirmed useful practices and arrangements. He presented decisions of the *Rule* and questionable points with keen result, as well as practices the *Rule* did not mention. Everyone gave assent. Benedict then prepared for the emperor a chapter by chapter decree for confirmation to enjoin observance in all monasteries of his realm. We refer the inquiring reader to that document.

36:2. Louis appointed inspectors for each monastery to oversee whether those practices that were enjoined were observed and to transmit the wholesome standard to those unaware of it. By the aid of divine mercy the work was happily accomplished. All monasteries were returned to a degree of unity as if taught by one teacher in one place. Uniform measure in drink and food, in vigils and singing, was decreed to be observed by all. Since Benedict established observance of the *Rule* throughout other monasteries, he instructed his own at Inde so that monks coming from other regions might not engage in the noisy conversation to which they were accustomed, but might see the standard and discipline of the *Rule* portrayed in usage, walk, and dress of the monks at Inde.

Chapter 37:1. Because of the indiscreet warmth of many, the unwarranted tepidness of some, and the obtuse sensibility of those with less capacity, Benedict determined a boundary and gave to all an arrangement to be observed, restraining some from seeking superfluous exertions, commanding others to shake off sluggishness, admonishing still others to fulfill at least what they did know. He ordered many things in conformity with the *Rule*. But there are a great many matters demanded in daily practice about which the *Rule* is silent. Yet by them a monk's habit is adorned as if with jewels and without which it appears to be careless, monotonous, and disorganized.

37:2. For the sake of unity and concord or perhaps for the sake of honorable appearance or even out of consideration for human frailty, Benedict commanded some matters that are not inculcated in the *Rule*.

Hence the venerable *abba* of holy memory ascertained what should be observed without delay or under pretext of excuse and ordered them fulfilled. Those matters which for certain reasons should be remitted or changed, he did not consider but entrusted them to his students to be observed in some measure as he could differentiate according to possibility or according to place. Where any page of the *Rule* explains less lucidly or remains altogether silent, he established and supplied with reason and aptness some matters on which, with divine help, I will touch briefly as follows.

Chapter 38:1. First, how the bell was to be rung for the night hours. Benedict ordered that a small bell in the brothers' dormitory be tapped, so that the congregation of monks maintained by prayer might first occupy their own place. Later,[74] when the doors of the church were opened, entry might be permitted to guests. Rising quickly, as the *Rule* orders, the brothers should sprinkle themselves with holy water and run humbly and reverently to all the altars, then go to their places so that when the third bell is rung they may stand without delay, with ears attuned, awaiting the priest designated to begin the office.

38:2. During this interval no one allowed to enter was permitted to stand in corners of the church, but stationed in choir they were to intone quietly the prescribed Psalms. Benedict ordered them to sing five Psalms for all the faithful living throughout the whole world; then five for all the faithful departed; and five for those who were recently deceased.[75] He decreed that the last five be sung comprehensively, for there was no reason regularly to mention specific deceased persons. When those last five Psalms were completed, one might prostrate himself in prayer, commending to

God those in general for whom he sang; and only then begin to petition for particular persons. As one's body lies on the earth there should be no reluctance to supplicate the eternal King in specially prescribed Psalms. One should not fear to bow his head at designated words along with others able to do so, since in this manner divine grace is suitably invoked and the warmth of compunction is aroused.

38:3. In summer time, when the office of Matins is over, Benedict ordered the monks to go outside the church if they were sleepy. Putting on their sandals and washing their faces, they could then return fully aroused and as before go around the altars with reverence, sprinkle themselves with holy water, and then go to the places allotted to each to complete the day office in an honorable manner, as well as those offices which are, according to Roman use, rendered with Psalm 118 [Ps. 119 in modern versions]. He ordered the bell to be rung a long time: while it was ringing everyone could rush, but when it stopped the priest was to begin the 'Hour.' When Prime was over, they could disperse to assemble in chapter. When that was completed, they could then go out to the task imposed on them either in silence or in singing Psalms. Those who remained at the monastery must not be occupied in idle stories [*fabulis . . . ociosis*][76] but two by two or even singly they were to sing Psalms whether in kitchen, mill, or cellar. But he decreed that after Compline no one might go outside freely or even linger in the oratory.

38:4 In winter time they should sing ten Psalms; in summer, five. Then, when the last bell is rung, all should walk together around all the altars in the aforesaid manner, and thereafter go to sleep, each on his own bed. At those three times each day he commanded them to go around all the altars. At the first one they should say the Lord's Prayer and the Creed; at the others, the Lord's Prayer; or they should confess their sins. At the day hours for prayer, each should go to his own place to pray. If, however, one had peculiar reason to pray alone, he should do so only by permission and only at whatever hour he was not otherwise occupied. Benedict established those three stations of prayer so that those who were sluggish, slow, or not in a mood to pray might at least do under compulsion what they did not want to do freely and thus not abandon the appointed hours, while those who were aflame with extreme love might be restrained from indiscreetly seeking extra hours. Thus it came to pass that they were not worn away with excessive or indiscreet vigils during the course of one night and hence preoccupied at the hours when one should be intent on divine Psalms, since one cannot fulfill the divine requirement while sleepy.

38:5. The practice of many had in the past caused them also to dress differently. The cowls of some hung down to their ankles. God's man therefore instituted a uniform style to be worn by all monks: the length should not extend more than two cubits or reach to the knees. Out of necessity he conceded beyond what the *Rule* decrees: two woolen shirts, pants, leather cloaks and coverings, and two copes. Whatever he observed as necessary to diminish evasion by any pretext, he conceded and allowed.

38:6. In a letter to the emperor, Benedict gave his opinion on those matters which the *Rule* directs but which for good reason remained untried, as well as on those matters on which it was silent but which were usefully introduced. He directed his desire toward observance of the *Rule*; it was his greatest study that nothing might escape his knowledge. Consequently he interrogated minutely those whom he found to be expert, whether living nearby or at a distance. Those who came into these parts on their way to Monte Cassino he asked to collect not only what they heard, but also what they saw. Because of his love of knowledge, anyone who might unfold something new to him he received without delay, with humility, and chatted with him without awe.

38:7. Even so he could not learn all the hidden meanings of the *Rule*. With everyone (not with novices, of course, but with wise persons) he would make it clear that he learned new and unheard of matters not only from learned people, but also from simpler ones. He caused a book to be compiled from the rules of various fathers, so that blessed Benedict's *Rule* might be foremost in the minds of all. He gave orders to read it all the time in the morning at assembly. To demonstrate to contentious persons that nothing worthless or useless was set forth by blessed Benedict, but that his *Rule* was sustained by the rules of others, he compiled another book of statements culled from other rules. To it he gave the title, *Harmony of the Rules*. Statements in agreement with blessed Benedict's book were added to show that the latter was obviously foremost. To it he joined another book from the sermons of holy teachers. These were presented for exhortation of monks. It he ordered read all the time at the evening assemblies.

Chapter 39:1. Perceiving that some men panted with all their might to acquire monasteries of monks and strove not only with petitions, but also with money, to obtain them; perceiving, too, that monastic expenses were being sequestered by them for selfish purposes; and perceiving that in that way some monasteries were being destroyed and others secured by secular clergy after the monks were driven away, Benedict went to the most pious emperor and pressed him with supplications to ban clergy from contentions of this kind and set the exiled monks free from this danger. The most glorious emperor gave consent and decreed that all monasteries in his realm where there were regular abbots be enumerated. By charter he ordered that they remain unchanged for all time; he sealed that charter with his ring. Thus he stripped the greed of many and at the same time relieved the anxiety of the monks.

39:2. Certain monasteries were employed for secular burdens and for military service. They had reached such dire poverty that both food and clothing were lacking to the monks. Considering that, the most pious king, at the aforesaid man's suggestion, gave order to relieve them as much as possible so that nothing might be lacking to God's servants. For this alleviation they gladly prayed to God for the emperor, his children, and the pious establishment of the entire realm. Those monasteries that remained under canonical authority he arranged separately so they could live according to the *Rule*, but the rest he granted to the abbot.

Chapter 40. I think I should not overlook what happened by God's will once when Benedict was going to a general diet at the emperor's order. Although worn by illness and severe fever, he was on his way in obedience to the king's order. Attended only by the weapons of charity, he was prepared to accomplish the benefit of many persons. But the enemy, who always envies holy deeds and seeks to bring detriment to the salvation of pious people, strove by any craft to slow him down on the path he had undertaken through vast forests. Driving away the horses on which Benedict was traveling, he confused the guides and rendered the way unfamiliar to them. But God's man was not discouraged by grief over the lost horses and he soon reached the royal gates. When the losses on the monasteries and monks were reported to the emperor, he, who had great, constant, and holy solicitude for them, replenished the number of horses. Yet after an interval of a month the lost horses were returned. Thus by divine action it came to pass that Benedict received double reward because he had not grieved over what was lost.

Chapter 41:1. Thereafter he began to wear away with differing ailments: the constant vigils through many years, streaming tears, severe fasts, and prolonged meditations. He undertook, therefore, to prepare his frail, worn body for a new struggle, so that he, who had gained the pinnacle of virtues by subduing vices, might be girded with weapons of patience to strive against infirmities and gain the victor's double palm from his King after his foes were overthrown. The more vigorously he was mauled by illness, the more intently he pursued over and over again prayers and readings. No one found him idle, no one found him sluggish at Divine Office, no one found him indulging in vain and frivolous stories [*frivolisque fabulis*].[77] He persisted either in reading by himself or in listening attentively to someone else reading.[78] Who ever found him alone except also weeping?[79] Who ever entered his place unannounced and found his cheeks dry and him not prostrate on the ground or standing with hands outstretched to heaven or catching his tears in his hands lest a page of the sacred volume be stained with them?

41:2. The powers of his flesh wasted, but his purpose of spirit was firmer than iron. He endured in the hardness he had begun. Not since the day of his conversion did Benedict eat the flesh of four-footed animals. Even in his last days when he was worn by listlessness he scarcely ever indulged in a bath. He was accustomed to change his clothes only after forty days or more.[80] He ordered brothers to read the life and death of the holy fathers to him. Refreshed by that reading his spirit endured even stronger. O good Jesus,[81] drenched with what sighs and tears did his spirit seethe with desire to be released and be with Messiah [cf. Phil. 1:23],[82] but he never refused to perform a duty if it was helpful to the brothers.

41:3. When illness grew stronger, he appealed directly to the emperor to be borne to his monastery. Delivering a farewell address to the brothers, he spent the whole night in prayers and Psalms, then went to the regular office of that day. On a later day when he completed the regular office and tried to reach the door, a phrase recurred to him, "You are upright, O Lord" [Ps. 119:137]. Reciting that versicle, he said, "I am fainting," and added, "Treat your servant, O Lord, according to your mercy" [Ps. 119:124]. Thus amid words of prayer he breathed out his spirit adorned with virtues.

Letters

41:4. His letters, sweeter than all riches, are here. The day before he departed from the world he dictated them with his own mouth to the brothers stationed at Aniane. In them he testified that they would see his face no more [cf. Acts 20:25, 38]. Certain ones declare that at the very hour he departed to Messiah, his death was revealed to Bishop Stabilis of Maguelonne. Rising from sleep the latter quickly related to his men what had occurred. We have, therefore, touched upon his death cursorily for brothers who were present at that time have unfolded it more extensively as the following pages indicate.

Chapter 42:1. [From the monks of Inde to Ardo] "Abbot Benedict, born in the province of Gothia, lived there from infancy to adolescence in the days of Pepin, king of the Franks, and after his death, in the days of his son Charles. Later abandoning the palace, he took the habit of a true monk at the monastery of Saint Seine in the province of Burgundy. There he served in God's knighthood[83] zealously for two and a half years.[84] But since he found little practice of the *Rule* there, he removed to the regions of Gothia. At first he built with his own hands a cell on the river Aniane and afterwards, with the help of brothers who for love of Messiah came under his government, a monastery of new foundation. Not long thereafter he had three hundred monks under his authority.

42:2. "When Emperor Charles died and his son Louis received the empire, the latter caused the venerable man Benedict to come with several students to Frankland. At first Louis granted Benedict Marmoutier in the countryside of Alsace, but later for love of him erected a completely new monastery for him on the river Inde near the palace of Aix. It was through Benedict that the Lord Messiah restored the *Rule* of Saint Benedict in the entire realm of the

Franks. He had under his government twelve monasteries: Aniane, Gellone, Casa Nova [Goudargues], Île-Barbe, Ménat, Saint Savinus, Saint Maximin, Massay, Cormery, Celleneuve near Toulouse, Marmoutier in Alsace, and Inde. The last was erected by the emperor's authority for Benedict and his students and endowed from the royal treasuries. For all these Benedict dispatched monks and abbots of his own teaching. He had the greatest concern for the entire ecclesiastical order, whether monks, canons, or layfolk, but especially for monks.

42:3. "The emperor listened to all his counsel willingly and accomplished it. For that reason Louis was called by some 'the Monkish.'[85] For love of the holy man he always called the monks 'his own' and after Benedict's decease he went so far as to declare himself openly 'abbot' of this monastery. The holy man continued up to his death in the king's palace for the benefit of all the faithful, although not for earthly profit. The monastery in which he dwelled was nearby. On the fourth day before his demise[86] and while he was still well he repeated to the emperor everything that he was in the habit of saying to him. On that day, however, he returned to his own dwelling wracked with fever. On the next day[87] all the emperor's magnates heard about that and came to visit him. So great was the throng of bishops, abbots, and monks that we, who were keeping watch over him, scarcely had space to get close to him. Abbot Helisachar came first and remained with him until he died.

42:4. "Benedict grew sicker on the fifth *feria*.[88] On the sixth *feria*[89] at nightfall the emperor sent Tanculf, his chamberlain, ordering that we should convey him that very night to the monastery. Lifting him up, we bore him before cockcrow in company with Helisachar, his men, and ours to the monastery at the first hour of the day [Prime]. When the third hour of the day [Terce] came, Benedict ordered everyone to leave him and he remained alone until the sixth hour [Sext].[90] After that Abbot Helisachar and our provost entered and inquired how he was feeling. He replied that he had never been so well and added, 'Until now I have been standing among the choirs of holy ones in the Lord's presence.' On the next day[91] he summoned the brothers, gave them reminders of salvation, then confided to them that in the forty-eight years since he had been a monk he had eaten no food on any day until he poured out tears before God.

42:5. "On the same day[92] he sent a note of admonition to the emperor and directed others to various monasteries. In them the venerable man noted every office he had performed during the five years and two months before his death, as we found in his records after his death. While still alive he spoke of certain offices to be sung for him. He died in his seventies on the third day before the Ides of February [i.e., on 11 Feb.],[93] in the year of the Lord's incarnation 821, the fourteenth indiction, first concurrent, fourteenth epact, ninth year[94] of most pious Emperor Louis. We prepared his grave on the third day[95] afterward and put him in a stone coffin that the emperor had had prepared.[96] As we covered his face, we noticed on the forehead, above his eyes, and on his lips such ruddiness as he never had while alive.

42:6. "These matters having been thus indicated and thus delivered, we, servants of the monastery of Inde, namely, Deidonus, Leovigild, Bertrad, and Desiderius, desire for you, Master Ardo, health in the

Lord and we beg your charity to compose and send to us, according to your God-given wisdom, a little book about the life of our Father Benedict. All our brothers greet you and do you greet all your brothers for us. Amen."

Chapter 43:1. [From Benedict to George] "For George, abbot of the monastery of Aniane, of supreme beatitude and felicity in the Lord Messiah, and for all our sons and brothers who live well and watchfully under the standard of Benedict, Benedict, least of all abbots, already at his end, desires health.

43:2. "Above all things and before all matters that burn my spirit and require care is this: that I am intensely solicitous for your order in the regular life. In no way am I unaware that you sweat nobly. You are loyally mindful of us and are in no wise wanting in words of encouragement. Set in my last stages, not knowing whether I can see you again, but since my love turns my spirit toward you, I have taken care to address some words to you through faithful persons as well as through letters. You know how with all possible labor I have availed as long as I could. Solicitous for you I have exhibited patterns of life and exhortation. Now, therefore, my sons, I pray to God and call Him to witness that you may be of one mind in the bond of charity [cf. Eph. 4:3] and that you may be discreet. Do not hold anyone as 'foreigner' whom I have had with me. I have not sent people anywhere to seek another example or another reason. Whoever may wish to return to you from among them and live with you under the *Rule*, you will receive in holiness and kindness as brothers, for that is fitting.

43:3. "Thanks to God, material aid will not fail you. To all in general, but especially to those whom you know to be joined with us in friendship, always offer an attentive disposition so far as you can. Minister to poorer monasteries the necessities that are more than sufficient for you. Give aid to Abbot Modan, of the monastery of Saint Thibery, in those matters in which he may be in want. After my death do even more for these and others than you did in my lifetime. Many monasteries are still corrupt even though they have, through God's largess, received some correction from us. So beware in every way lest (may it not be!) — I pray you, merciful Lord — the sinister way . . . that may be able to hold at all times. You at the monastery of Inde, be united as very special brothers.

43:4. "Consider Helisachar (who before others upon earth has always been a loyal friend of canons) and his brothers in my place and may your refuge always be in him. I now advise you thus because I do not know whether I may see you again in this present world. Already on the seventh day before the Ides of February [i.e., on 7 Feb.][97] with a very sharp pain, Messiah granting His mercy . . . I am smitten. I await nothing other than the last day of my summons speedily."

43:5. Lord Benedict ordered the foregoing to be written on the fourth day before the Ides of February [i.e., on 10 Feb.][98] while he was still living. He died on the third day before the Ides of the same month [i.e., on 11 Feb.][99] Here ends the letter.

43:6. The divine seed has been sown; may it avail
            for new ones,
        Drenched with dew from heaven, to plow the
        planting of teachers,
        And the rich field of the heart produce fruit
        a hundredfold [cf. Mark 4:8].[100]

Chapter 44. [From Benedict to Nibridius] "Abbot

Benedict, least of all abbots, to Archbishop Nibridius, venerable father in Messiah, I wish health and eternal felicity in the Lord. O man of God, may charity, love, and good will be evident now as always. By yourself in person or through a servant or friend transmit a message throughout all monasteries wherever you can, that they not cease to pour out prayers for me to the Lord together with Psalms and Masses, because such intercession is now profoundly necessary for me. Know, beloved father, that I am now struggling at my end, that my soul has left my body, and that I can no longer see you in the light with eyes of the body. May He who can make a clean person out of an unclean one, a just person out of a sinner, and a holy one out of an irreligious person, cause us to enjoy the eternal realm there to sing the new song with all the holy ones [cf. Rev. 14:3].

44:2. "I beg, dear father, that as you have always had an interest in the brothers dwelling at the Aniane monastery, so always keep them more and more in your holy love until your holy soul leaves your body. I commend to you all my friends, servants, and relatives in those areas. In your own monastery, I believe, you work with all your efforts. Be zealous to labor for them with perseverance. Ever use your mouth to all, rich and poor alike, in accord with that statement which the Lord deigned to speak through His blessed Apostle Paul, 'Declare, implore, scold' [II Tim 4:2]. May your holiness know well to whom to declare, whom to implore, and whom to scold. I therefore say to you, father, may no peril remain in you whereby you might be forever damned. With free voice may you be able to say with the Psalmist, 'I have not hidden away your uprightness in my heart, but I have uttered your truth and your salvation' [Ps. 40:10]. Do everything, however, with charity and discretion. May the Holy Trinity guard you and grant you bountifully the eternal reward. Amen."

Notes to Introduction

1 The day, month, and year are given in the text as indicated. The day of the week was determined by use of Erich Bornmann, *Zeitrechnung und Kirchenjahr* and *Calendarium perpetuum* (Kassel: J. Stauda, 1964). Watkin Williams, "St Benedict of Aniane," *Downside Review*, LIV (July 1936), 374, says Friday.

2 Allen Cabaniss, *Charlemagne* (New York: Twayne Publishers, inc., 1972), 18f.

3 The anonymous life of Louis, I, 6:1, as translated in Allen Cabaniss, *Son of Charlemagne* (Syracuse: Syracuse University Press, 1961), 37; Allen Cabaniss, *Judith Augusta: A Daughter-in-Law of Charlemagne, and Other Essays* (New York: Vantage Press, 1974), 18.

4 Williams, "St Benedict of Aniane," 359f. See earlier Sigurd Abel, *Jahrbücher des fränkischen Reichs unter Karl dem Grossen*, I, 2nd ed. B. Simson (Leipzig: Duncker und Humblot, 1888), 439f.

5 SS, I, 31.

6 Ibid., 300.

7 Allen Cabaniss, "Felix of Urgel, Archheretic," in his *Judith Augusta*, 67; originally published as "The Heresiarch Felix," *Catholic Historical Review*, XXXIX, No. 2 (July 1953), 129-141.

8 Ibid., 69.

9 See J. Böhmer, E. Mühlbacher, J. Lechner, *Die Regesten des Kaiserreichs unter den Karolingern 751-918* (Innsbruck: Verlag der Wagner'schen Universitäts-Buch-handlung, 1908), No. 318. Hereinafter this work will be cited as Mühlbacher, *Regesta*.

10 Ibid., No. 340.

11 There were three gatherings at Aix-la-Chapelle: Aug. 816, July 817, and July 818; see David Knowles, *From Pachomius to Ignatius* (Oxford: Clarendon Press, 1966), 8. But cf. Josef Semmler, "Die Beschluss des Aachener Konzils im Jahr 816," *Zeitschrift für Kirchengeschichte*, LXXIV (1963).

12 His name is given as Aigulf by Herbert Thurston and Donald Attwater, *Butler's Lives of the Saints*, I (New York: P.J. Kenedy and Sons, 1956), 309.

13 The Latin word is *sutor*, which Williams, "St Benedict of Aniane," 358, renders as *tailor*.

14 Allen Cabaniss, "Bodo-Eleazar, Convert to Judaism," in *Judith Augusta*, 106-122; originally published as "Bodo-Eleazar: A Famous Jewish Convert," *Jewish Quarterly Review*, XLIII, No. 4 (Apr. 1953), 318-328.

15 Ermoldus Nigellus, *In honorem Hludowici*, II, line 555, in PLAC, II, 40.

16 Erwin Panofsky, *Abbot Suger on the Abbey Church of St.-Denis and its Art Treasures* (Princeton: Princeton University Press, 1946), *passim*, especially 63.

17 The Latin is *scientia scripturarum peritos*, not simply "those expert in written compositions," *pace* Arthur J. Zuckerman, *A Jewish Princedom in Feudal France 768-900* (New York: Columbia University Press, 1972), 212.

18 And see his letter to his student Guarnarius, EppKA, II 561-563.

19 Edmund Bishop, "On the Origin of the Prymer," in his *Liturgica Historica* (Oxford: Clarendon Press, 1918), 211-237, especially 211-214, 236f.

20 Twelve foundations are listed in Ardo's *Vita Benedicti* as indicated, but Josef Semmler, "Karl der Grosse und das Fränkische Mönchtum," in Wolfgang Braunfels, ed., *Karl der Grosse: Lebenswerk und Nachleben*, II (Düsseldorf: L. Schwann, 1965), 255-289, especially 260, adds a possible thirteenth and suggests that thirty-eight others were strongly influenced by Benedict.

21 The quotation is from Pierre Tisset, *L'Abbaye de Gellone au diocèse de Lodève des origines au XIIIe siècle* (Paris: Recueil Sirey, 1933), 3.

22 SS, I, 301.

23 PL 133:53D-54A.

24 See Barnard S. Bachrach, "A Reassessment of Visigothic Jewish Policy," *American Historical Review*, LXXVIII, No. 1 (Feb. 1973), 11-34.

25 Eleanor S. Duckett, *Alcuin, Friend of Charlemagne: His World and His Work* (New York: Macmillan Co., 1951); Max Manitius, *Geschichte der lateinischen Literatur des Mittelalters*, I (Munich: Beck, 1911), 273-288.

26 Alcuin, Epistola 56, EppKA, II, 99f.

27 Epistola 57, ibid., 100f.

28 Epistola 184, ibid., 309f.

29 Epistola 200, ibid., 330-333.

30 Epistola 201, ibid., 333f.

31 Epistola 205, ibid., 340-342.

32 Epistola 206, ibid., 342f.

33 Epistola 207, ibid., 343-345. Alcuin addressed

H

also Epistola 303, ibid., 461f., to Nibridius and Benedict, exhorting them to assiduity in their labors.

34 *Vita Alcuini*, 19 (SS, XV, Part I, 184-197).

35 Ibid., *prologus*.

36 Manitius, *Geschichte*, I, 537-543.

37 Theodulf, Carmen XXX, "Ad monachos sancti Benedicti," PLAC, I, 520-522. The quotation above is from lines 23f. Other lines will be cited internally.

38 Allen Cabaniss, *Agobard of Lyons: Churchman and Critic* (Syracuse: Syracuse University Press, 1953), 4. The latest book on Agobard is Egon Boshof, *Erzbischof Agobard von Lyon: Leben und Werk* (Vienna: Böhlau Verlag, 1969); on which see my remarks in *Catholic Historical Review*, Oct. 1974, 480f.

39 Bishop, *Liturgica Historica*, 333-348 (as in note 19).

40 See Cabaniss, *Charlemagne* (as in note 2).

41 See Cabaniss, *Son of Charlemagne* (as in note 3).

42 Ibid., 81.

43 See Cabaniss, "Felix of Urgel" (as in note 7).

44 Benedict probably knew both empresses. On Judith, see Cabaniss, *Judith Augusta* (as in note 7).

45 PL 103:393D-702.

46 Ibid., 703A-1380B.

47 Ibid., 1419B-1431A.

48 EppKA, II, 561-563.

49 Bishop, *Liturgica Historica*, 213.

50 David Knowles, *The Monastic Order in England* (Cambridge: University Press, 1949), 28, note 2.

51 *Pace* Williams, "St Benedict of Aniane," 358.

52 The anonymous life of Louis, III, 44, 45, 48-53, in Cabaniss, *Son of Charlemagne*, 89-92, 95-105 (as in note 3 above).

53 See note 15 above. Ermoldus's poem in four books was edited by Ernst Dümmler in PLAC, II, 5-79; a later ed. and trans., Ermold le Noir, *Poème sur Louis le Pieux et épitres au roi Pepin*, was prepared by Edmond Faral (Paris: Champion, 1932). Manitius, *Geschichte*, 554f., has some useful bibliography.

54 M.L.W. Laistner, *Thought and Letters in Western Europe, A.D. 500 to 900*, 2nd ed. (Ithaca, N.Y.: Cornell University Press, 1957; first published, 1931), 356.

55 See note 53 above. My internal citations are from the PLAC edition.

56 Although not supported by any MS, this word could be *agnatus* (born). In any case Benedict was born about eighteen years before Louis the Pious.

57 See preceding note.

58 Williams, "St Benedict of Aniane," 357, "some eight miles."

59 Wilhelm Pückert, *Aniane und Gellone* (Leipzig: Hinrichs'che Buchhandlung, 1899), especially chapters 1, 3, and 4.

60 On Tisset, see note 21 above, especially chapters 1, 2, and 5.

61 Joseph Bedier, *Les legendes épiques: recherches sur la formation des chansons de geste*, I, *Le cycle de Guillaume d'Orange*, 3rd ed. (Paris: Édouard Champion, 1926), especially chapters 3, 4, and 5.

62 See reviews by Bernard S. Bachrach, *American Historical Review*, Dec. 1973, 1440f., and by Allen Cabaniss, *Catholic Historical Review*, July 1973, 317-319.

63 Paschasius Radbertus, *Vita Walae*, II, 8:4, as translated in Allen Cabaniss, *Charlemagne's Cousins* (Syracuse: Syracuse University Press, 1967), 161.

64 Probably the most extensive treatment is Joseph Calmette, *De Bernardo s. Guillelmi filio (?-844)* (Toulouse: Privat, 1902), *passim*. But see also Léonce Auzias, *L'Aquitaine carolingienne (778-987)* (Paris: Didier, 1937), 37; Zuckerman, *A Jewish Princedom* (as in note 17 above), 122, 184; E. Hlawitschka, "Die Vorfahren Karls des Grossen," in Braunfels, *Karl der Grosse* (as in note 20 above), I, 51-82, especially 77.

65 The year is given in *Chronicon Moissiacense* (as in note 6 above).

66 Bibliographical details in note 17 above.

67 Zuckerman, *A Jewish Princedom*, 207, note 82.

68 Ibid., 208 and note 84, citing and adding to Pückert, *Aniane und Gellone* (as in note 59 above), 109, note 8.

69 Ibid., 211.

70 Ibid. My rendering is sustained by Williams, "St Benedict of Aniane," 364. Similar faulty proofreading by Zuckerman occurs on pp. 243f., where he has *Bernard* instead of the correct *Benedict*; see note 91 below.

71 Zuckerman, *A Jewish Princedom*, 212.

72 Ibid.

73 Ibid.

74 Ibid., 223.

75 Ibid., 224, note 115; but see Paschasius, *Vita Walae*, II, 6:1; 19:1 (Cabaniss, *Charlemagne's Cousins*, 157, 192).

76 Paschasius, *Vita Walae*, I, 3:5; 6:5; II, 1:2; 9:7; 15:4 (Cabaniss, *Charlemagne's Cousins*, 93, 100, 149, 167, 182).

77 Zuckerman, *A Jewish Princedom*, 240, note 148; see Allen Cabaniss, "Popular Revolt in the Ninth Century," *Studies in English*, XIII (1972), 111-118.

78 Cf. the amusing "tale of Abbot John" by Fulbert, bishop of Chartres (fl. 1007), about the monk who wanted to live *sicut angelus* (like an angel), but repented after a week of effort, *cum angelus non potuit, vir bonus esse didicit* (since he could not be an angel, he learned how to be a good man). F.J.E. Raby, ed., *The Oxford Book of Medieval Latin Verse*, 2nd ed. (Oxford: Clarendon Press, 1959), 180-182.

79 Karl Young, *The Drama of the Medieval Church*, I (Oxford: Clarendon Press, 1933), 201. See also Allen Cabaniss, *Amalarius of Metz* (Amsterdam: North-Holland Publishing Co., 1954), 64f.

80 Urban T. Holmes, Jr., in Holmes and M. Amelia Klenke, *Chrétien, Troyes, and the Grail* (Chapel Hill, N.C.: University of North Carolina Press, 1959), 51-61.

81 See Cabaniss, "Bodo-Eleazar," as in note 14 above.

82 Cited by Zuckerman, *A Jewish Princedom*, 238-241.

83 Ibid., 241.

84 See Cabaniss, *Agobard of Lyons*, 63-71 (as in note 38 above).

85 Zuckerman, *A Jewish Princedom*, 242.

86 The Latin is ambiguous: it may be read as above or as, "leaving behind no trace of worldly ostentation." Logic virtually demands this latter version, which is rendered in French by Bedier, *Les legendes épiques*, I (as in note 61 above), 113, "sans plus garder aucun vestige des pompes mondaines." Yet grammatically and verbally the reading given in the text above is not only possible, but also probable. What it really means, I do not know, but cf. the unambiguous statement in 35:2, *seculari pompa relicta* (secular pomp abandoned).

87 Thegan, *Vita Hludowici*, 36, in Reinhold Rau, *Fontes ad historiam regni Francorum aevi Karolini illustrandam*, I (Berlin: Rütten und Loening, 1956), 236.

88 Zuckerman, *A Jewish Princedom*, 217, note 98.

89 See Allen Cabaniss, "France's First Woman of Letters," in *Judith Augusta* (as in note 7 above), 52; originally published as "The Woes of Dhuoda," *Mississippi Quarterly*, XI, No. 1 (Winter 1958), 38-49.

90 Zuckerman, *A Jewish Princedom*, 239, note 144.

91 Ibid., 244. Here and on the preceding page Zuckerman substituted the name *Bernard* for *Benedict*.

92 See his *From Pachomius to Ignatius* (as in note 11 above), 8.

Notes to Text

1 See introduction B above. I have bypassed the possibility that Ardo may also have been known as Smaragdus, not to be confused with a later person of that name.

2 The oldest *Life of St. Gregory the Great*, by a monk of Whitby, XXX, alludes to "our small ability." See Charles W. Jones, *Saints' Lives and Chronicles in Early England* (Ithaca, N.Y.: Cornell University Press, 1947), 118.

3 Sulpicius Severus, *Life of St. Martin, Bishop of Tours*, dedication, expressing fear that unpolished diction might prove displeasing to a reader. See. F.R. Hoare, *The Western Fathers* (New York: Sheed and Ward, 1954), 10.

4 Perhaps vague Vergilian allusions.

5 Sulpicius, *St. Martin*, dedication (Hoare, *Western Fathers*, 10), asks reader to pay attention to matter rather than to language.

6 See 38:3; 41:1 below; cf. Paschasius Radbertus, *Adalard*, 2; 4:2; *Wala*, I, 5:4, 5, 6 (Cabaniss, *Charlemagne's Cousins*, 26f., 96f.).

7 Sulpicius, *St. Martin*, dedication, as in note 3 above.

8 We would employ the plural, but medievals

111

stressed the singular; see Gregory of Tours, *Liber vitae patrum*, SS. rer. Merow., I, 662f.

9 Sulpicius, *St. Martin*, preface (Hoare, *Western Fathers*, 10), to rouse a desire for true wisdom.

10 Ibid., dedication (Hoare, *Western Fathers*, 10), when asked so often, the author cannot refuse.

11 See introduction A:28 above.

12 See 41:4; 43:1-4 below.

13 Sulpicius, *St. Martin*, dedication (Hoare, *Western Fathers*, 10).

14 See introduction A above.

15 Sulpicius, *St. Martin*, II (Hoare, *Western Fathers*, 12), his father, beginning life as common soldier, rose to office of military tribune.

16 Ibid., II (ibid., 14), won the hearts of his fellow soldiers.

17 Ibid., II(ibid., 13), was a cavalryman under Emperor Justinian and later under Caesar Julian.

18 Felix, *Life of St. Guthlac*, XVIII (Jones, *Saints' Lives*, 133), "a spiritual flame began to burn."

19 Sulpicius, *St. Martin*, III (Hoare, *Western Fathers*, 15), Martin continued in his military service, but only in name, for nearly two years after baptism; *Gregory the Great*, II (Jones, *Saints' Lives*, 98), thought it better to cling to secular dress.

20 Felix, *St. Guthlac*, XXXIII (Jones, *Saints' Lives*, 141), "our athlete of Christ."

21 It is strange that the author does not reveal whether the attempt was successful.

22 See 3:1; 42:1.

23 Constantius, *Life of St. Germanus*, IV (Hoare, *Western Fathers*, 289), only bedclothes were a piece of sacking.

24 Ibid., could get little sleep in such discomfort.

25 Sulpicius, *St. Martin*, II (Hoare, *Western Fathers*, 13), cleaning his servant's boots.

26 Constantius, *St. Germanus*, IV (Hoare, *Western Fathers*, 289), garments used, unless one was given away, until they fell apart from wear.

27 Ibid.

28 Sulpicius, *St. Martin*, III (Hoare, *Western Fathers*, 15), laughter from bystanders at his grotesque look in ragged garments.

29 For a definition of compunction, see Grimlaic, *Regula solitariorum*, 29 (PL 103:617D), "Compunctio etenim cordis est humilitas mentis cum lacrymis et recordatione peccatorum et timore judicii" (Compunction of heart is humility of mind together with tears, remembrance of sins, and fear of judgment). See also ibid., 30 (ibid., 618D), "Duo igitur sunt compunctionum genera hoc est irriguum superius et irriguum inferius. Irriguum quippe inferius accipit cum inferni supplicia flendo pertimescit. Irriguum vero superius accipit cum sese in lacrymis coelestis regni desiderio affligit" (There are two kinds of compunction, namely, one watered from above; the other, from below. Whoever shudders and weeps at the punishments of hell has the compunction watered from below. But he who melts in tears at desire for the kingdom of heaven has the compunction watered from above).

30 Felix, *St. Guthlac*, XXXII (Jones, *Saints' Lives*, 141), same reference to Gehenna.

31 Constantius, *St. Germanus*, III (Hoare, *Western Fathers*, 288), took a taste of ashes before eating his barley bread.

32 See introduction A:9 above and Knowles, *From Pachomius to Ignatius*, 3-5.

114

33 See note 20 above.

34 This sentence alludes to the Benedictine *Rule*, 3, on the duties of cellarer to the sick, children, guests, and poor.

35 See 2:3 above and 42:1 below.

36 See introduction A:27.

37 Cf. Vergil, *Aeneid*, IV, 173-177.

38 See introduction A:4.

39 Ibid.

40 Precisely the same story is told of Alcuin, *Vita Alcuini*, 19, and in similar words. For the same kind of story, see Sulpicius, *St. Martin*, XIV (Hoare, *Western Fathers*, 28).

41 *Gregory the Great*, X (Jones, *Saints' Lives*, 104), has a miraculous story about a locust; cf. the strange account of a plague of locusts by St. Augustine, on which see Allen Cabaniss, "Two Notes on Augustine, Charlemagne, and Romance," *Augustinian Studies*, V (1974), 77.

42 *Gregory the Great*, IV (Jones, *Saints' Lives*, 99), cites the same passage of Scripture.

43 Sulpicius, *St. Martin*, X (Hoare, *Western Fathers*, 25), many of his students become bishops.

44 Mühlbacher, *Regesta*, No. 318, dated 27 July 792.

45 Ibid., No. 349, June 799.

46 A council in Arles, May 813, convoked by the emperor.

47 The word *declinarat* probably implies disapproval.

48 "Giving away raisins" (*palmas caedere*), but this translation may not be accurate.

49 See introduction C:3 (c).

50 Felix, *St. Guthlac*, XLV (Jones, *Saints' Lives*,

150), left no one without consolation even though melancholy.

51 See introduction A:27.

52 Cf. preceding note.

53 Only the letters cited in introduction A:25 have been preserved.

54 Constantius, *St. Germanus*, XII (Hoare, *Western Fathers*, 296f.), same kind of miracle.

55 Sulpicius, *St. Martin*, XII (Hoare, *Western Fathers*, 26), turning around in ridiculous whirligigs; cf. the folk story of the mad dancers of Kolbeck.

56 *Gregory the Great*, XVIII (Hoare, *Western Fathers*, 107), "But, to return to the subject."

57 Notice the unusual title.

58 Cf. 36:1 below.

59 Sulpicius, *St. Martin*, IX (Hoare, *Western Fathers*, 23).

60 See introduction C:2.

61 Ibid., 8.

62 His sons: Bernard and Gaucelm.

63 See introduction C:11 and note.

64 Cf. 28:2 above and note 56 above.

65 The queen may have been Irmingard, Louis's first wife, or Judith, his second, or both.

66 I have preserved the Aramaic *abba* here and at the other places where it appears in Latin: 35:2; 37:2.

67 *Chronicon Moissiacense*, 814 (SS, I, 311), and Ermoldus Nigellus, *In honorem Hludowici*, II, 555f.

68 No longer extant.

69 Note the use of military terminology for monastic service.

70 An interesting sidelight on Louis's nervousness.

71 The same for his forgetfulness.

72 Cf. 29:1 above.

116

73 See introduction A:5 and note.

74 Ardo numbers the first and third bells, but not the second.

75 The gradual Psalms 120-134.

76 Cf. (f) above and 41:1 below.

77 Cf. (f) and 38:3 above.

78 Cf. 2:4 above.

79 *Gregory the Great*, XXIX (Jones, *Saints' Lives*, 117), Gregory entered the church and wept copiously.

80 Cf. 2:4 above.

81 Cf. this exclamation in Paschasius, *Wala*, I, 21:8 (Cabaniss, *Charlemagne's Cousins*, 132).

82 *Gregory the Great*, XXXII (Hoare, *Western Fathers* 120f.), same citation of Scripture.

83 Cf. note 69 above.

84 See 2:3 and 3:1 above.

85 Probably used only here of Louis.

86 Fri., 8 Feb. 821.

87 Sat., 9 Feb. 821.

88 The fifth feria is Thursday. Apparently there is some repetition or discrepancy here.

89 The sixth feria is Friday.

90 These seem to be references to the appropriate hours of Divine Office of Saturday.

91 This is Sun., 10 Feb. 821.

92 Still Sun., 10 Feb. 821.

93 Mon., 11 Feb. 821.

94 Counting from Louis's first coronation in 813.

95 "On the third day," i.e., two days later, Wedn., 13 Feb. 821.

96 Felix, *St. Guthlac*, XLVIII (Jones, *Saints' Lives*, 152), Abbess Ecberga, daughter of King Aldulf, made for Guthlac a leaden coffin with the request that he be interred in it.

97 Thurs., 7 Feb. 821.
98 Sun., 10 Feb. 821.
99 Mon, 11 Feb. 821.
100 These three hexameters were probably composed by some brother at Inde, not by Ardo.

Brief Index of Names